FireFighterPrep's Comprehensive Guide to Canadian Fire Fighter Exams

COMPREHENSIVE GUIDE TO CANADIAN FIRE FIGHTER EXAMS, published by:

FireFighterPrep
http://www.firefighterprep.com
info@firefighterprep.com

Authors:
Deland Jessop, Kalpesh Rathod, and Adam Cooper.

ISBN 978-0-9735151-6-9

Printed and bound in Canada

Table of Contents

Introduction

Welcome to FireFighterPrep. We understand the situation you're in and the challenges you face ahead. This study guide was developed to help you prepare for many of the Fire Service exams used by fire departments across Canada.

By purchasing this guide, you have taken an important step - you have moved from thinking about doing something to improve your chances of being hired to taking action. Fire Departments are looking for action-oriented individuals. Your dedication to preparing for your exams demonstrates that you are just this type of person.

If you are looking for more practice tests and further preparation materials, visit our website at WWW.FIREFIGHTERPREP.COM. We offer a special discount of 25% for those who have purchased this guide. If you're interested in taking advantage of this offer, input the following code into the Referral Code section when registering on our website (note the code is case sensitive):

ppdc0745

Please do not hesitate to contact us if you have any questions, concerns or comments about this book, our website, or the application and testing process. We will be happy to assist you in any way that we can.

Email: info@firefighterprep.com
URL: http://www.firefighterprep.com

Preparation Material

Resume Building

A resume is a tool used to demonstrate your suitability for the job-specific requirements of a career. This holds true with fire fighting. Few people have received instruction on building a resume, or had much experience writing them. They don't understand what should or should not be included to present themselves in the best manner they can.

Resume building does not start at the writing stage. If you are serious about becoming a fire fighter, you should have a long list of volunteer experience, academic achievements, languages, computer skills and other highlights to place on your resume. If you don't, begin today. Many organizations, including food banks, charity organizations and Children's Aid Societies are desperate for volunteer help. Languages are becoming more important to fire departments, as are computer skills and many other life skills.

The main purpose of your resume is to frame your experiences, skills and knowledge in a manner relevant to the fire service to which you are applying. You have to not only demonstrate what you've done, but also show that you have done it well. It is crucial to present information clearly and concisely so the person reviewing your resume can quickly find what they require. Three principles should be followed:

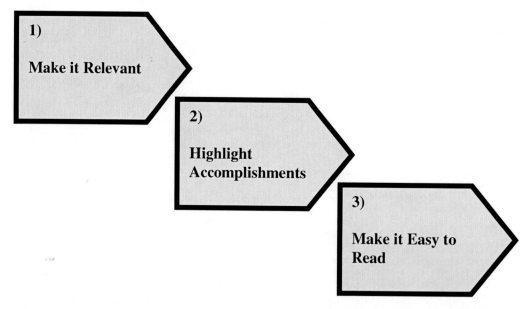

1) Make it Relevant

2) Highlight Accomplishments

3) Make it Easy to Read

Principle One: Make it Relevant

Fire services want to fill positions with people who fit their needs. It is important to determine what competencies are required for the job. Below is a list of core competencies that fire services are searching for.

Analytical Thinking	The ability to analyze situations and events in a logical way, and to organize the parts of a problem systematically.

Self – Confidence	A belief in your capabilities and recognition of personal limitations.
Communication	You must have the skills to effectively communicate using listening skills and verbal and written communications skills.
Flexibility / Valuing Diversity	As a fire fighter, you will have to work with a wide cross-section of the community that includes diverse backgrounds, cultures and socio-economic circumstances. You must have the ability to adapt your approach to each situation.
Self - Control	Firefighting can be extremely stressful. You must establish that you can control your emotions actions when provoked.
Relationship Building	Developing contacts and relationships both within and outside the fire service is extremely valuable.
Achievement Orientation	You must demonstrate a desire for continuous improvement in service and accomplishments.
Concern for Safety	The ability to exercise caution in hazardous situations in order to ensure safety to self and others.
Assertiveness	The capacity to use authority confidently and to set and enforce rules appropriately.
Initiative	Demonstrated proficiency to be self-motivated and self-directed in identifying and addressing important issues.
Cooperation	Willing to act with others by seeking their input, encouraging their participation and sharing information.
Community Service Orientation	Proven commitment to helping or serving others.

Commitment to Learning	Demonstrated pattern of activities that contribute to personal and professional growth.
Organization Awareness	A capacity for understanding the dynamics of organizations, including the formal and informal cultures and decision-making processes.
Developing Others	Commitment to helping others improve their skills.

Many people squeeze everything into a resume hoping that something will click. Any material on your resume that does not exhibit traits from the list of core competencies the fire service is looking for is a waste of space.

Do not include every employer on your resume unless you are specifically asked to provide that information. Many fire services require an employment history application. Pick out the most relevant positions you have had and focus on demonstrating the qualities. Any additional information such as Activities, Volunteer Experience, Education, or Special Skills should also demonstrate your competencies.

Basic Qualifications

Ensure that you have the basic qualifications covered in your resume or application process for whatever fire department you are applying for. Below are some common examples.

- Legally entitled to work in Canada
- Ontario Class D driver's license
- Strong command of the English language
- Willingness to work shifts (days / nights / weekends / holidays)
- Between the ages of 18 and 60 years

- Grade 12 education or equivalent
- "Z" air brake endorsement
- Full pardon for criminal convictions

On top of the above basic requirements, any of the following skills are valued highly by fire departments.

- Any technical trade
- SCUBA certification
- Building inspection / Plans development
- Military / Coast Guard
- Radio / Communication systems operator
- CPR instructor certificates
- Swimming experience / Lifeguard

- College or University education
- Volunteer firefighting
- Public Service (Police, Nurse, Paramedic)
- Environment application
- Computer / IT skills and training
- Outdoor pursuit skills
- Climbing experience

Principle Two: Highlight Accomplishments

Accomplishment statements should give the fire service an indication of how well you performed. It should reveal not only what you did, but also how well you did it. Each statement should include the following:

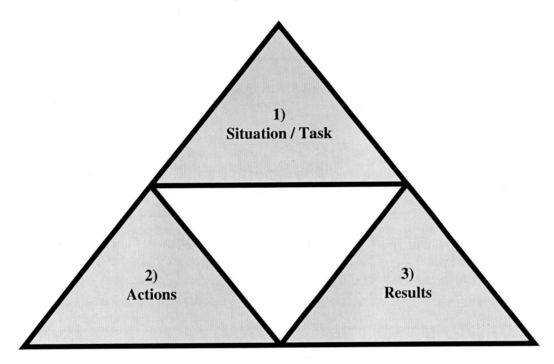

Each accomplishment statement should describe skills relevant to the fire service. Practice writing these statements. Typically, accomplishment statements fall under the Work Experience, Volunteer Experience, or Education sections of your resume.

Each statement should use action verbs that emphasize and empower your accomplishment statements. Quantifying your results when you can will add impact.

Example Action Statements

1) Day Camp Counsellor

Core Competency	Situation / Task	Action	Result
Developing Others, Cooperation, Concern for Safety, Assertiveness, Community Service, Communication.	Field trips as a day camp counsellor.	Instruction and supervision.	Ensured safety of 60 children with fellow counsellors.

"Supervised and instructed 60 young children on field trips, ensuring their safety and enjoyment with a team of fellow counsellors."

2) Retail / Grocery

Core Competency	Situation / Task	Action	Result
Work Organization, Communication, Negotiation / Facilitation	Controlling Inventory.	Organized units and placed orders (quantified)	Diverse customer needs anticipated and satisfied.

"Organized shelving units and placed orders in excess of $20,000, ensuring diverse customer needs were anticipated and satisfied."

3) Post-Secondary Education

Core Competency	Situation / Task	Action	Result
Initiative, Achievement Orientation, Analytical Thinking, Commitment to Learning, Communication	Attending post-secondary education.	Studied sociology (or any other major)	Graduated with a strong standing, developing a core set of skills.

"Developed analytical, presentation, computer and XXXX skills by studying sociology, graduating with a 75% average."

4) Volunteer Work

Core Competency	Situation / Task	Action	Result
Initiative, Communication, Cooperation, Work Organization, Developing Others, Self-Confidence, Flexibility / Valuing Diversity, Negotiation / Facilitation, Community Service Orientation	Food drive at work.	Organized and implemented.	Raised $2,000 for needy people in the community.

"Organized and implemented a Food Drive with a team of volunteers, effectively raising $2,000 for needy people in the community."

Action Verbs to be used for your Accomplishment Statements			
Accelerated	Displayed	Negotiated	Saved
Accumulated	Documented	Ordered	Scheduled
Accomplished	Effected	Organized	Selected
Acquired	Enforced	Performed	Separated
Analyzed	Engineered	Perpetuated	Served
Applied	Evaluated	Planned	Set
Arranged	Facilitated	Prepared	Shared
Assessed	Filed	Prescribed	Showed
Authorized	Financed	Presented	Solved
Approved	Founded	Problem-solved	Strengthened
Began	Generated	Processed	Succeeded
Bought	Hired	Produced	Supplied
Budgeted	Identified	Promoted	Taught
Coached	Implemented	Provided	Team-built
Collected	Invented	Questioned	Trained
Combined	Launched	Raised	Translated
Communicated	Learned	Read	Tutored
Conducted	Made	Realized	Uncovered
Convinced	Maintained	Reorganized	Unified
Coordinated	Managed	Repaired	Utilized
Developed	Marketed	Researched	Vitalized
Directed	Minimized	Revised	Won
Discovered	Monitored	Risked	Wrote

Principle 3 - Make it Easy to Read

Fire recruiters look at thousands of resumes each year. They do not necessarily spend a lot of time on each one. This means your resume has only a few minutes to prove that you are a good fit for their service. The information presented has to be immediately pertinent and easy to read. Key things you should be mindful of when finishing up your resume are:

- use high quality bond paper
- incorporate as much white space as possible so the reader is not overwhelmed
- highlight only key words or positions to attract attention
- use bullet points rather than paragraphs
- keep font sizes between 10 and 12 pt

Language and grammar are very important on a resume and the following should be observed:

- make every word count
- use short, simple and concrete words that are easily understood
- use strong nouns and vital verbs to add action, power and interest
- avoid personal pronouns
- spell check the document and always have someone proof read the material
- double check the meaning of easily confused words, i.e.:

> affect (influence) vs. effect (result)
> personal (private) vs. personnel (staff)
> elicit (draw forth) vs. illicit (unlawful)
> discreet (showing good judgement) vs. discrete (distinct or separate)
> allude (indirect reference) vs. elude (to evade)

A few rules-of-thumb

- months do not need to be included in dates when the length of employment is greater than six months
- part-time and full-time descriptors are generally not included
- do not include names of supervisors
- check with the fire service you are applying to about disclosing full employment history

Review the copy of the sample resume below.

Resume Components

Name	Address Telephone Number E-mail

Education

Educational Institution Location Degree	Date
Educational Institution Location Degree	Date

Work Experience

Company, Geographic Location Position title - Descriptive Statement if needed - Relevant Accomplishment Statement - Relevant Accomplishment Statement	Date
Company, Geographic Location Position title - Descriptive Statement if needed - Relevant Accomplishment Statement - Relevant Accomplishment Statement	Date
Company, Geographic Location Position title - Descriptive Statement if needed - Relevant Accomplishment Statement - Relevant Accomplishment Statement	Date

Examples of Optional Section Headings

- Professional Development
- Computer Skills
- Languages
- Activities and Interests
- Volunteer Experience

- Awards
- Summary of Qualifications
- Functional Skills
- Publications
- Academic Achievements

Jane / John Doe (EXAMPLE)
123 Main St # 1, Anytown Ontario A1A 1A1 (416) 555 - 1212
jdoe@x.com

Education

CITY COLLEGE, Toronto, Ontario   (2001 -2004)
Fire Services Diploma
- Elected Class President and managed a budget of $5,000 and a team of 15 volunteers to deliver class social activities and educational assistance programs.

MAIN STREET COLLEGIATE, Toronto, Ontario   (1997-2001)
OSSD, OAC Certificate, Honour Roll, Senior English Award

Professional Experience

Hammersmith Gas Company, Toronto, Ontario   (2004-present)
Gas Technician
- Installed furnaces, air conditioners and boilers in both residential and commercial units.
- Responded to emergency situations including potential gas leaks and equipment malfunctions.

Toronto Parks Department, Toronto, Ontario   (2000-2002)
Assistant Activity Implementer
- Scheduled and implemented a variety of after school activities for 50 – 60 children with fellow co-workers.
- Used a needs-based approach to assist children from diverse cultural backgrounds with a variety of problems, such as schoolwork, bullying and loneliness.

Volunteer
- Thanksgiving Food Drive - annually delivering food to needy people throughout the community
- Children's Aid Society – Special Buddy Program   (2000-2002)
- City College Orientation Leader   (2002)

Interests
- Centre for Toronto Vikings ice hockey team.   (2002-2004)
- Short stop for Beaches Marlins Baseball team.   (2000-2005)
- Certified SCUBA Diver   (present)
- Basic Rescuer or Level "C" CPR certificate and First Aid Certificate

Computer Skills
- Excel, WordPerfect, PowerPoint
- Internet development, Outlook

The Interview

It is important to recognize that fire services are looking for the best people for the job and will not try to consciously confuse you.

At this stage it is your interpersonal and communication skills that will help you land a job with the fire service. The interviewer is looking for someone who is competent, likeable and who fits in with the organization's culture, goals, beliefs and values.

What Interviewers Tend to Look For

Friendly Personality

As a firefighter, you spend a great deal of time with co-workers. You effectively live at the fire station with your co-workers. Every interviewer will be asking themselves whether or not they could stand to work with you for an entire shift. You must prove that you are likeable enough to do this.

Organizational Fit

Fire services have a particular culture and it is important for interviewers to ensure that job applicants will fit into that culture. Suitability includes a willingness to work shift work and overtime if required, attend community events to speak about fire safety, and an ability to function well as a member of a team. There is a list of other competencies outlined in the Resume Section.

It is important not to pretend to be something you're not. If you feel you wouldn't fit in with a firefighting culture, then it is probably best for both you and the organization that you seek another career. It is important to ask these questions of yourself. Once in the interview stage, you should be confident that you would fit in with the culture.

Capable and Professional

Fire services want competent personnel. A great deal of authority and responsibility comes with this job. You must demonstrate that you are capable of handling the responsibility and that you can perform under pressure. Again, it is important to review the core competencies outlined in the Resume Section.

Handling Pre-Interview Stress

Feeling nervous before an interview is perfectly normal. Politicians, entertainers and media personalities feel nervous prior to performances as well. The best way to handle the stress is to be well prepared. Once again, interviewers are not trying to trick you. They want you to succeed; it makes their job easier. Some things you should do before the interview include:

- Get a good night's sleep (this goes without saying, but bears repeating).
- Practice interviewing with friends, using the material below.
- Wear professional clothing (suits or business dress).

You should bring all of the documents that the fire service requests of you (transcripts, copy of your resume, portfolio) to the interview along with a pad of paper, a pen, a list of references and a list of questions you may have. Interviewers are often impressed if you have intelligent and researched questions about the job.

How to Influence the Hiring Decision

Understand the Fire Service – THIS IS EXTREMELY IMPORTANT

It is important to have at least a rudimentary understanding of the fire service to which you are applying. This information is available on most websites, or at the stations and employment office of the fire service. Some information you should know would include:

- Rough size of the service (example: Niagara Falls has about 100 full-time professional firefighters and 100 volunteer – 2002).
- Name of the commanding officer (example: Alan Speed – Toronto 2002).
- Areas of service (example: Niagara Falls covers over 81 square miles).
- Community specific issues that affect the fire department. For example, Vancouver is a very ethnically diverse community where language barriers may exist. Hamilton is a region, which includes both light and heavy industry. Calgary is a rapidly growing city with a great deal of on-going construction.
- The challenge that all municipal services are facing (asked to do more with less, biohazard training, threats of terrorism, etc.)

Before any interview, read the local newspaper of the community you are applying to for several weeks so that you are aware of the local issues and concerns.

Understand the Job

You have to understand that the job of a firefighter is not just fighting fires and tending to emergency situations. If asked a question about the daily duties of a firefighter, you have to include as many of the roles as possible. Include:

- Ongoing training

- Maintaining and cleaning equipment
- Interacting with the public and developing community relations
- Filling out paper work and reports
- Public education
- Tours
- Fire prevention
- Inspections (smoke alarms in buildings).

You should also point out that firefighting is a 24 / 7 / 365 job – 24 hours a day, 7 days a week, 365 days a year. Mention that you have a duty to act in emergency situations you come across while off duty. This could include a child choking at a family picnic, children playing with matches in the park, to coming across a fire while driving home from work.

First Impressions

First impressions are extremely important. Many judgements are made about a person within the first 30 seconds of an encounter (fairly or unfairly). It is your job to impress the interviewer(s). Three basic steps you can take to ensure that you make a great first impression are:

Look Professional	Be Confident	Break the Ice
Interviewers want to see an applicant who respects them enough to wear the appropriate attire.	Greet the interviewer(s) with a smile, a firm handshake, a relaxed manner and a friendly "Hello".	Engage in small talk. It can be about anything, (weather, traffic, etc). It doesn't have to be profound. It's meant to put both parties at ease.

Communication and Interpersonal Effectiveness

The interview process is a situation that tests your communication skills. You should be aware of the following:

Eye Contact	Maintain eye contact with the person you are addressing. This means looking at the person who is speaking to you. In interviews with more than one interviewer spend an equal amount of time on each person.

Body Language	Be aware of your position in your seat and your breathing pattern. Attempt to relax by taking steady breaths. Make sure you sit up straight in an interview. This will exhibit self-confidence and professionalism.
Gestures and Speech	Be aware of any gestures you use. Nod and maintain eye contact to indicate that you understand interview questions. Smile when appropriate, and be vocally expressive by alternating your tone where necessary. Be natural and avoid filler words such as "umm" and "like".

During the Interview

Make an effort to read the interviewers. Ask yourself whether they appear to be straining to follow you, if you are talking too fast (breathe more deeply), or too softly (speak louder). If they are writing frantically, that is usually a good sign, but make occasional pauses so that they can keep up. If you do not understand a question, ask them to repeat or clarify it. If you do not know the answer to one of their questions, admit it. Do not lie during the interview.

Prepare Stories Prior to the Interview

Interviewers may have some questions regarding your resume, or your past experiences. Make sure you are familiar with the content in your resume, and any tasks that you mention in it.

Interviewing Methods

There is a strong possibility that you will be asked technical or "what if" questions or questions about your past. Some fire departments will ask questions such as:

- What would you do if you caught a fellow co-worker stealing property at a fire?
- Have you ever smoked marijuana?
- Could you risk your life to save another?
- Have you ever committed an illegal act?
- You are told to evacuate a building and an old lady doesn't respond to your orders. What would you do?
    - o Question whether it's a language barrier, shock, an injury etc.
    - o Coax her, talk to her, wave to her, lead her by the arm, call for assistance.
    - o If necessary pick her up and carry her down.

It is important to give these questions careful consideration and answer honestly. If you tried smoking marijuana when you were in high school, admit it and tell the interviewer why you didn't continue to use it. For example, you found it hurt the academic performance of your friends, or something along those lines.

"What if" questions are intended to challenge you, to see if you are the type of person who will immediately back down. This is not a trait the fire service is looking for. Once you have made up your mind on an issue, stand by it. Interviewers may challenge you but this is part of the process. Just ensure that you give careful thought to the question to avoid defending a weak position. It is acceptable to credit the other opinion, but do not change your decision.

How to Answer Behavioural Based Questions

Many fire services will use a behavioural-based interview method. This means that they will ask you questions about yourself and will ask you to describe events that have actually occurred in your past (usually in the last two years). Some examples of questions you should be prepared to answer include:

Give an example in your life when you:

- were involved in a stressful situation and how you dealt with it.
- were extremely angry and how you dealt with it.
- had to take the role of a leader, and how was the situation resolved.
- had to work as part of a team and explain what happened.
- had to resolve a conflict with other parties and how did you handled it.
- were up against an important deadline and how you handled the work.
- had a conflict with a supervisor and how you handled it.

There are many other behavioural questions, but these are some common examples used by fire services.

Each behavioural question is a story about your past. Make sure that the story you tell is relevant, clear, and even interesting (interviewers are only human). Each story should have:

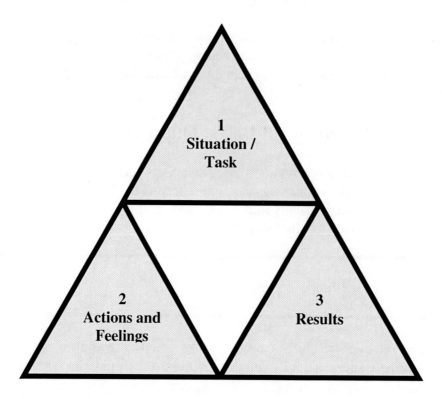

Step One - Understand the Question

This is vital. If you do not understand the question or what the interviewer is asking for, ask them to repeat it or explain it. There is no point giving a very effective answer to the wrong question. For example: one interviewee, asked about Ethnicity, spoke a great deal about Ethics during an interview. The interviewers probably thought he was an idiot, but he was probably just nervous and didn't hear the question properly.

Step Two - Brief Synopsis

Let the interviewers know what you plan to talk about with a brief outline of the situation, with little detail. This will give you some time to organize your thoughts and the interviewers will understand where you are going. This should take no longer than a couple of sentences.

Example:

"I am going to tell you about a conflict I had with my boss while I was working as a personal trainer. It involved a situation where I was told to bill a client at a rate I didn't feel was justified. We dealt with it away from the customer and resolved it in a manner that satisfied myself, the manager, and the client."

Step Three - Full Story

A retelling of the story will demonstrate to the interviewers your competencies in dealing with the situation and your communication capabilities. Interviewers want a clear story, preferably in a chronological sequence. They are most concerned with your feelings during the situation, the actions you took, and the result of your actions. Always finish the story with the results of your actions. Keep these points in mind both while you are preparing for the interview, and when you are participating in it:

- Answer the question asked.
- Pause and think – don't rush in with an answer.
- Pay attention to the pronouns you are using. Interviewers want to know what "YOU" did. Use the pronoun "I" for your actions and "Us" for team actions. **DO NOT ALWAYS USE "WE".** You will fail the interview.

Bad Example:
"We formed a team to solve the problem. We brainstormed an idea to solve the problem. We then decided on a course of action and began to implement it. We handled task "A" while others handled task "B". We all had individual assignments."

Good Example:
"I formed a team to solve a problem. We brainstormed an idea to solve the problem. I then had to decide the course of action and we began to implement the solution. My friend John and I were responsible for task "A" while another group handled task "B". My particular assignment was to do "X".

- **Ensure you effectively explain the situation, your feelings, your actions and the result.**
- If necessary take pauses to collect your thoughts. There is no need to be constantly talking.
- Relax and enjoy telling the story. You should know it well, as you actually did it.
- Give focused and fluid answers.
- Avoid run-on answers.
- Give support for claims that are made, if possible.
- Show evidence of preparation work.

Completing the Interview

Just like the first impression, it is important to give a positive impression during the last few moments of an interview. If you have any questions for the interviewers, the end of the interview is when they should be asked. It is acceptable to have prepared questions written down. As you are leaving the room, smile at the interviewer(s) individually, walk up to each one, look into their eyes, shake their hands and personally thank them for their time.

General Suggestions

Preparation Prior to Testing

Check out the websites and contact the fire service for which you are interviewing to ensure that you are familiar with the testing procedures and the content of the exams. Tests are often standardized but individual services may have variations. It is important to get as much information as possible from the department to which you are applying.

Practice on numerous tests to ensure that you are familiar with the content of the testing material. Get enough sleep before the tests and enough food and water even if you are nervous. Try to remain relaxed and comfortable. Wear clothing that is professional but also comfortable to work in. If you are doing physical testing on the same day, you may want to wear athletic gear. Arrive early and ready to begin.

During the Test

Sit close to the front of the testing area, so that you will better hear any recordings played for memory tests.

Don't waste time on a question you are unable to answer; take a guess and move onto the next question. Make a note of answers you are not certain of, and review them if you have time after answering the remaining questions.

Pay attention to the answer sheet and the question number. Many applicants have failed as the result of an error on the scoring card. Every time you respond to a question, look at the answer card carefully and make sure that the number you are answering on the card matches the number of the question.

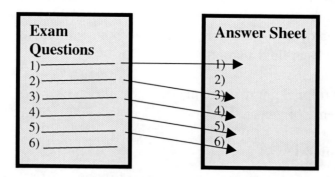

In the above example, even if the applicant answered the questions correctly, he or she would only get one out of the six questions right because of the errors on the scoring card. Keep this in mind when taking the test. Because they are computer scored, you will not be able to correct or explain yourself if you make a mistake on the answer sheet. This mistake is more common if you decide to skip a particular question. If you do, avoid making an order error by crossing off the question you skipped on the answer card.

Teaching Material
Math

Addition

$$
\begin{array}{r}
7 \\
+ \quad 5 \\
\hline
12
\end{array}
\qquad\qquad 7 + 5 = 12
$$

The above two equations have the same value and are very straightforward. It is important to know that the order of numbers does not make a difference in addition (or multiplication). For example:

$$
\begin{array}{r}
6 \\
+ \quad 3 \\
\hline
9
\end{array}
\qquad \text{same} \qquad
\begin{array}{r}
3 \\
+ \quad 6 \\
\hline
9
\end{array}
$$

$$243 + 716 = 959$$
$$\text{same}$$
$$716 + 243 = 959$$

Some complications arise when larger numbers are used and you need to carry numbers.

Note: When you see a math problem laid out horizontally, as in the box immediately above, rearrange the numbers so that they are vertical (on top of each other) to make the addition easier to do.

Example:

$$
\begin{array}{r}
3\,5\,1 \\
6\,9\,9 \\
+4\,5\,7
\end{array}
$$

(A) **(B)** **(C)**

(A)	(B)	(C)
3 5 1	▸1 3 5 1	▸2 3 5 1
6 9 9	6 9 9	6 9 9
+ 4 5 7	+ 4 5 7	+ 4 5 7
17	20 7	15 0 7

(A)
Start by adding up the numbers in the right most column. The result is 17. The seven remains but the one is carried over to be added to the next column of numbers.

(B)
The same rules apply to the sum 20 in the second column. The 0 remains in the second row, while the 2 is carried over to the column to the left to be added.

(C)
The final column is then added and the answer is recorded.

Subtraction

$$
\begin{array}{r}
8 \\
-\quad 3 \\
\hline
5
\end{array}
\qquad 8 - 3 = 5
$$

The above two equations have the same value and are very straightforward. It is important to know that the order of numbers is significant in subtraction (and division). Different ordering will result in different answers. For example:

$$
\begin{array}{r}
18 \\
-\quad 3 \\
\hline
15
\end{array}
\quad \text{different} \quad
\begin{array}{r}
3 \\
-\ 18 \\
\hline
-\ 15
\end{array}
$$

$$712 - 245 = \quad 467$$
$$\text{different}$$
$$245 - 712 = -467$$

Some complications arise when larger numbers are used and you need to carry numbers.

Example:

$$
\begin{array}{r}
7\ 4\ 3 \\
-\ 5\ 8\ 9 \\
\hline
\end{array}
$$

(A)

$$
\begin{array}{r}
3 \\
7\ {}^{4}1\,3 \\
-\ 5\ 8\ 9 \\
\hline
4
\end{array}
$$

(B)

$$
\begin{array}{r}
6\quad 13 \\
7\ 4\ 3 \\
-\ 5\ 8\ 9 \\
\hline
1\ 5\ 4
\end{array}
$$

(A)
The first task is to subtract the right most column. Because 9 is larger than 3, a unit has to be borrowed from the column to the left. The 4 in the middle column is reduced to 3, and the one is added to the right column, making the first row 13 - 9 = 4.

(B)
The second task is to subtract the second column. The same process is repeated. Borrow a 1 from the left column to allow the subtraction. The top number in the left column becomes 6, while the top number in the centre column becomes 13. 13 - 8 = 5. The left column would then be subtracted. 6 - 5 = 1.

Note: If subtracting more than 2 numbers, you cannot stack the numbers as you would in addition. Instead, work from the first subtraction to the last, two numbers at a time.

Multiplication

$$
\begin{array}{r}
8 \\
\times \quad 6 \\
\hline
48
\end{array}
\qquad 8 \times 6 = 48
$$

The above two equations have the same value and are very straightforward. It is important to know that the order of numbers makes no difference in multiplication (or addition). For example:

$$
\begin{array}{r}
7 \\
\times \quad 8 \\
\hline
56
\end{array}
\qquad \text{same} \qquad
\begin{array}{r}
8 \\
\times \quad 7 \\
\hline
56
\end{array}
$$

$$245 \times 233 = 57{,}085$$
$$\text{same}$$
$$233 \times 245 = 57{,}085$$

Multiplication, simply put, is adding groups of numbers. For instance, in the above example, the number 8 is being added six times.

$8 \times 6 = 48$	$7 \times 7 = 49$
$8 + 8 + 8 + 8 + 8 + 8 = 48$	$7 + 7 + 7 + 7 + 7 + 7 + 7 = 49$
$9 \times 5 = 45$	$6 \times 3 = 18$
$9 + 9 + 9 + 9 + 9 = 45$	$6 + 6 + 6 = 18$

It will be difficult to pass a fire exam if you have to calculate all simple multiplication in this manner. You should memorize the basic multiplication tables for 1 through 12. Review the multiplication table in this book.

Some complications arise when larger numbers are used and you need to carry numbers.

Example:

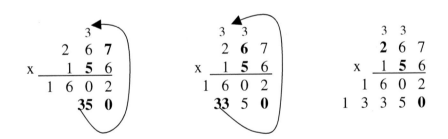

(A)
Begin by multiplying out the right row. The 2 is recorded in the right column and the 4 is transferred to the middle column and recorded as above.

(B)
The second step is to multiply the 6 in the middle column. 6 x 6 = 36. The 4 that was carried over from step A has to be added to the 36. The result is 40 and the 0 is recorded in the middle column. The four is then carried forward to left column as in step A.

(C)
The 6 then has to be multiplied to the left digit on the top number. 6 x 2 = 12. The four that was carried over from step B is added to the 12. The result is 16 and recorded as shown.

(D-F)
The next steps are to multiply the second digit in the bottom row (the 5) to each of the top digits. The 5 is multiplied to the 7, the 6 and the 2. The process is the same as steps A - C. If the number is 10 or larger the number is carried over, as above, and added to the next multiplication.

It is important to remember that the next multiplication set has to be recorded on the line below and lined up starting in the next column. Place a zero in the right column to ensure the digits line up properly

	(G)				(H)				(I)		
		2	6	**7**		2	**6**	7		**2**	6	7
x		**1**	5	6	x		**1**	5	6	x		**1**	5	6
		1	6	0	2		1	6	0	2		1	6	0	2
	1	3	3	5	**0**	1	3	3	5	**0**	1	3	3	5	**0**
			7	**0**	**0**		**6**	**7**	**0**	**0**	**2**	**6**	**7**	**0**	**0**

The next steps are to multiply the left digit in the bottom number by each of the digits in the top number. The same process is used as outlined above if numbers have to be carried over.

Lining up of the digits is also necessary at this stage. Because you are multiplying from the hundreds column (the left most) you begin recording the answer in the hundreds column. Follow the same procedure as outlined above. Fill in the first two columns with zeros.

```
        2  6  7
   x    1  5  6
        1  6  0  2
     1  3  3  5  0
  +  2  6  7  0  0
     4  1  6  5  2
```

The final step is to add up the three numbers that were multiplied out. Treat the addition of these three numbers exactly as you would a regular addition problem. If you failed to line the numbers up properly, you will wind up with an incorrect answer. 41,652 is the final answer.

Note: Because complex multiplication questions (like the one above) involve addition, make sure you have a firm grasp of the addition section before trying to tackle multiplication.

Things to Watch For

Watch out for a multiplication question where the first digit in the bottom number is a zero, or where there are zeros in the equation. You still have to properly line up the digits. Note the highlighted zeros.

```
      3 4 5
  x       5 0
  1 7 2 5 0
```

Remember that zero multiplied by any other number is zero. In this situation you begin multiplying with the 10's column (the 5). Because you are multiplying from the 10's column, you begin recording your answer there. Place a zero in the first column.

```
        3
      6 0 9
  x         4
    2 4 3 6
```

When the four is multiplied to the 0, the result is 0. The number, which is carried over from multiplying 9 x 4 has to be added to 0, which results in the highlighted answer - 3.

```
      4 5 2
  x   3 0 9
      4 0 6 8
+ 1 3 5 6 0 0
  1 3 9 6 6 8
```

In this situation there is no need to multiply the bottom ten's digit out, as the result will equal 0. You must, however, properly line up the numbers. Because the 3 is in the hundred's column, you must begin recording your answer in the hundred's column. That is why there are two highlighted zeros.

Multiplication Tables

	1	2	3	4	5	6	7	8	9	10	11	12
1	1	2	3	4	5	6	7	8	9	10	11	12
2	2	4	6	8	10	12	14	16	18	20	22	24
3	3	6	9	12	15	18	21	24	27	30	33	36
4	4	8	12	16	20	24	28	32	36	40	44	48
5	5	10	15	20	25	30	35	40	45	50	55	60
6	6	12	18	24	30	36	42	48	54	60	66	72
7	7	14	21	28	35	42	49	56	63	70	77	84
8	8	16	24	32	40	48	56	64	72	80	88	96
9	9	18	27	36	45	54	63	72	81	90	99	108
10	10	20	30	40	50	60	70	80	90	100	110	120
11	11	22	33	44	55	66	77	88	99	110	121	132
12	12	24	36	48	60	72	84	96	108	120	132	144

Use of the Table

To use this table, take a number along the top axis and multiply it by a number along the side axis. Where they intersect is the answer to the equation. An example of this is 7 x 3. If you find 7 on the side axis and follow the row until you reach the 3 column on the top axis, you will find the answer – 21.

Look for simple patterns to assist your memorization efforts. For example:

Whenever 10 is multiplied to another number, just add a zero.

    10 x 3 = 30   10 x 7 = 70

    10 x 10 = 100   10 x 12 = 120

Whenever 11 is multiplied by a number less than 9, just double the digit 11 is multiplied by.

    11 x 3 = 33   11 x 5 = 55

    11 x 7 = 77   11 x 9 = 99

One multiplied by any other number is always equal to that number.

    1 x 1 = 1   1 x 4 = 4

    1 x 8 = 8   1 x 12 = 12

Zero multiplied to any number is always zero.

    0 x 10 = 0   0 x 3 = 0

Nine multiplied by any number less than 11 adds up to 9.

    9 x 3 = 27   (2 + 7 = 9)

    9 x 9 = 81   (8 + 1 = 9)

Division

$$6 / 3 = 2 \qquad\qquad 6 \div 3 = 2$$

$$\frac{6}{3} = 2 \qquad\qquad 3\overline{)6}\,^2$$

The above equations have the same values and are very straightforward. It is important to know that the order of the numbers is significant in division (and subtraction). Different ordering of numbers will result in different answers. For example:

$10 / 5 = 2$	different	$5 / 10 = 0.5$
$15 \div 5 = 3$	different	$5 \div 15 = 0.33$
$\dfrac{100}{10} = 10$	different	$\dfrac{10}{100} = 0.1$
$10\overline{)50}\,^5$	different	$50\overline{)10}\,^{0.2}$

Simply put, division determines how many times a number will fit into another. Picture an auditorium with 100 chairs available. Several schools want to send 20 students to see a play in the auditorium. Now you need to determine how many schools can attend the play. This will require division.

By dividing 100 by 20 ($100 \div 20$) you come up with the number 5. Five schools can send 20 students to attend the play.

Long Division

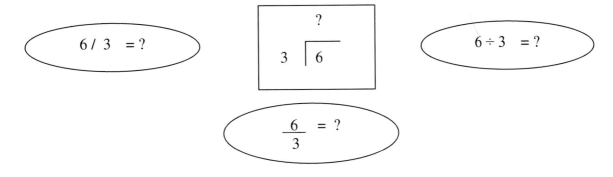

When performing long division, it is important to organize the information as is seen in the centre square. You have to understand how the different formats for division are transferred into the format seen above.

Example

$2653 \div 7 = ?$

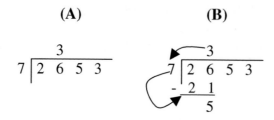

In order to answer a division question on paper, you must place the equation in the proper format. After this is accomplished you can begin to solve the problem.

(A)   **(B)**

(A)

The first step is to focus on the highlighted area of the number under the bracket. You have to work with a number that is larger than the dividing number (7). Because 2 is smaller than 7, you have to work with 26. Ask yourself how many times you can multiply 7 without going over 26. If you count by 7's (7, 14, 21, 28) you'll realize that 3 is the most times that 7 will fit into 26.

(B)

With the information you have in section A, you now have to perform a simple multiplication. Take the top number (3) and multiply it by the dividing number (7). The answer is placed below 26 and then subtracted from the digits you were working with. (26 - 21 = 5) Make sure you keep the numbers in the proper columns. (If, after subtracting, the answer is greater than the dividing number, you need to start again using a larger top number.)

(C)   **(D)**

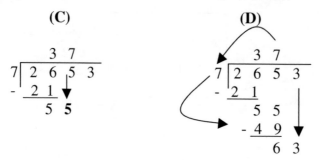

(C)

After subtraction, bring down the next digit to sit beside the solution. This becomes your new number to work with (55). Then repeat step A using this number. Determine how many times you can multiply 7 without exceeding 55. Place this digit above the next digit in the question on top of the bracket.

(D)

Next repeat step B. Multiply out the 7's and record your answer below the 55. Subtracting the numbers results in 6. Continue to work the same pattern, and bring down the next digit in the question to determine a new number to work with.

(E)

```
            3 7 9
    7 | 2 6 5 3
      - 2 1
          5 5
        - 4 9
            6 3
          - 6 3
              0
```

(E)

The final steps in the process are to repeat the process. Determine how many times you can multiply 7 without going over 63. You can do this 9 times. When you multiply it out and subtract the result is 0. The answer to the question is shown above.

$$2653 \div 7 = 379$$

Decimals

There are times when you are dividing a number and, after the final subtraction, there is a value left over. This is a remainder. When this happens, you can choose whether or not to continue calculating the number. If you continue, 1 or more decimal points will be introduced.

Example:

```
        3 3 1
    8 | 2 6 5 3
      - 2 4
          2 5
        - 2 4
            1 3
          - 0 8
              5
```

```
        3 3 1 . 6 2 5
    8 | 2 6 5 3 . 0 0 0
      - 2 4
          2 5
        - 2 4
            1 3
          - 0 8
              5 0
            - 4 8
                2 0
              - 1 6
                  4 0
                - 4 0
                    0
```

You must follow the same procedure with decimal places as you would with regular long division. Ensure that the digits are properly lined up, and continue adding 0's after the decimal places in the equation.

Decimals and Whole Numbers

You may be required to solve division problems with decimals already in place. Below are two examples of decimals occurring in division questions.

Example 1

```
    5 | 3 5 . 8 5
```

```
            7 . 1 7
    5 | 3 5 . 8 5
```

To answer the question correctly, you have to place the decimal point in the answer directly above the decimal point in the question.

Example 2

```
    2.7 | 2 8 6 2
```

```
               1 0 6 0 . 0
    27 | 2 8 6 2 0 . 0
```

When a decimal point is found in the denominator (the number of parts into which the whole is divided – bottom number of a fraction), then you must eliminate it before answering the question. This is achieved by shifting the decimal point however many spaces to the right it takes to create a whole number, in this example one space. This has to be matched by shifting the decimal place in the numerator (the number to be divided – top number of a fraction) by one space as well. If the numerator is a whole number, shift the decimal point right by adding a zero, as in the example above.

Example 3

$$3.5 \overline{)46.55} \qquad 35 \overline{)465.5} \;\; 13.3$$

When a decimal point is found in both the numerator and the denominator you must combine both steps. First, you must eliminate the decimal place in the denominator, as in example 2. Then you have to ensure that the new decimal place lines up, as in example 1.

Hints

Long division becomes more complicated with higher numbers, especially higher denominators.

$$67 \overline{)3015} \;\; 0045$$
$$-268$$
$$335$$
$$-335$$
$$0$$

Using 0's to Line up Numbers

67 will not fit into 3, or 30. You will therefore have to work with 301. By placing 0's above the 3 and the 0, (highlighted), you will not make any errors with improperly aligned numbers.

Rounding Up

Determining how many times 67 will fit into 301 can be a difficult task. It may help to round 67 up to 70. By counting 70 four times, you will reach 280. Five times equals 350, which exceeds 301. Four is the best guess, and by multiplying it out, using 67 you are proven correct.

Disregarding Decimals

The majority of the answers on a fire test will not require decimals. If your calculation of an equation gives you an answer with decimals, but none of the optional answers have decimals, stop calculating. Make a selection from the available options, or consider that you made a mistake. Quickly check your work, but don't spend too much time on one question that's causing you problems. Move onto the next question.

Zeros and Ones

Any time zero is divided by any other number the answer is 0.

$$0 / 3 = 0 \qquad 0 \div 25 = 0 \qquad \frac{0}{99} = 0 \qquad 0\overline{)99} \; 0$$

It is impossible for a number to be divided by 0. It is indefinable.

$$9 / 0 = \text{undefined} \qquad 77 \div 0 = \text{undefined} \qquad \frac{66}{0} = \text{undefined}$$

Any number divided by 1 is equal to itself.

$$3 / 1 = 3 \qquad 55 \div 1 = 55 \qquad \frac{1{,}297}{1} = 1{,}297 \qquad 1\overline{)38} \; 38$$

Place Value

It is important to maintain proper place value of digits when performing mathematical calculations. You must be able to convert written numbers into digits. For example:

Two million, forty thousand and two   2,040,002
One and a half million   1,500,000
Ten thousand and ten   10,010

You can practice place value questions by answering questions such as the ones below:

a) Write a number that is 100 more than 4, 904.
b) Write a number that is 1000 less than 478, 243.
c) What number is one more than 9,999?
d) What is the value of 5 in the number 241, 598?
e) What figure is in the ten thousands place in 4,365,243?
f) What number is 30,000 less than 423,599?

The answers are listed below.

Place value is important when lining up numbers for addition and subtraction questions. For example:

$$
\begin{array}{r}
20,602 \\
1,043 \\
603 \\
\underline{15} \\
22,263
\end{array}
$$

15 + 1043 + 603 + 20,602 =

$$
\begin{array}{r}
206.000 \\
13.090 \\
0.400 \\
\underline{0.002} \\
219.492
\end{array}
$$

13.09 + 0.4 + 206 + 0.002 =

One of the most common errors is failing to place digits correctly under one another, which often occurs when trying to calculate these problems in your head.

Answers to practice questions.

a) 5,004   b) 477,243

c) 10,000   d) 500

e) 6   f) 393,599

Make sure you are comfortable with the proper names for the location of digits in a number.

$$1,234,567.890$$

1 = millions column   2 = hundred thousands column

3 = ten thousands column   4 = thousands column

5 = hundreds column   6 = tens column

7 = ones column   8 = tenths column

9 = hundredths column   0 = thousandths column

Order of Operations

The following rules have to be obeyed while working with mathematical equations. There is an order to how numbers are manipulated and worked on.

B E D M A S

You should memorize this acronym, as it tells you how to proceed with an equation.

1)   **B** – Brackets

You must perform all mathematical calculations that occur within brackets before any other calculation in the equation.

2)   **E** – Exponents

After calculations within brackets are handled, you have to perform any calculations with exponents next.

3)   **D / M** – Division and Multiplication

Division and multiplication components are next. These are handled in the order they appear reading from left to right.

4)   **A / S** – Addition and Subtraction

The final calculations are individual addition and subtraction questions, which are performed in the order they appear reading from left to right.

The best way to understand this process is to work through several problems.

Example 1:		
$6 + 5 \times 3 - 7$	Step 1: Multiplication	$5 \times 3 = 15$
$6 + 15 - 7$	Step 2: Addition	$6 + 15 = 21$
$21 - 7$	Step 3: Subtraction	$21 - 7 = 14$
Example 2:		
$14 - 7 + 18 \div 3$	Step 1: Division	$18 \div 3 = 6$
$14 - 7 + 6$	Step 2: Subtraction	$14 - 7 = 7$
$7 + 6$	Step 3: Addition	$7 + 6 = 13$

Example 3:

$7 + (15 - 6 \times 2)$	Step 1: Brackets Remember to follow the order of operation within the brackets. (Multiply before subtracting.)	$6 \times 2 = 12$
$7 + (15 - 12)$		$15 - 12 = 3$
$7 + 3$	Step 2: Addition	$7 + 3 = 10$

Example 4:

$2 (2 + 5)^2$	Step 1: Brackets	$2 + 5 = 7$
$2 (7)^2$	Step 2: Exponents	$7^2 = 7 \times 7 = 49$
$2 (49)$	Step 3: Multiplication	$2 \times 49 = 98$

Remember that two numbers separated only by brackets are multiplied together (a bracket = x.) $2 (6) = 6 \times 2$

Practice Questions

Try these practice questions to see if you are comfortable with mathematical order of operation. The final answers are listed below.

a) $7 - 4 + 6 \times 8 \div 2$ b) $14 + 8 (6 - 3)$

c) $30 - 3(5 - 2)^2$ d) $(5 - 1) (4 + 7)$

e) $75 - (6 \div (2+1))^2$ f) $10^2 - 10 + 3^2$

g) $(10 + 3) \times 2 + 6(5-2)$ h) $17 + 6^2 (18 \div 9)$

i) $4 (5+2-3+6)$ j) $10 (6 + (15 - (10-5)))$

Answers

a) 27	b) 38	c) 3	d) 44
e) 71	f) 99	g) 44	h) 89
i) 40	j) 160		

Grouping Like Terms

You will come across mathematical problems where you have to group like terms together. Examples of this are very common with money. Whenever you are adding sums of money, there is no need to continually restate the same denominations. Below is an example of an equation adding up a suspect's money:

Denomination	# of Bills
$50	4
$20	3
$10	4

One means of calculating the total value of money seized is to individually add up all of the bills.

$$50 + 50 + 50 + 50 + 20 + 20 + 20 + 10 + 10 + 10 + 10$$

However, there is an easier and more orderly way of writing and working with this equation. Here is the statement rewritten separating the like terms.

$$(50 + 50 + 50 + 50) + (20 + 20 + 20) + (10 + 10 + 10 + 10)$$

Instead of adding all of the $50 bills together you can count the number of 50's and multiply that number by the value.

50 + 50 + 50 + 50	=	4 x 50 or 4 (50)
20 + 20 + 20	=	3 x 20 or 3 (20)
10 + 10 + 10 + 10	=	4 x 10 or 4 (10)

The statement can then be written more clearly as: $4(50) + 3(20) + 4(10)$

Remember that it doesn't matter what order the terms are in, so long as they remain together. The above equation could be restated any of the following ways:

$3(20) + 4(50) + 4(10)$ $20(3) + 50(4) + 10(4)$

$20(3) + 10(4) + 50(4)$ $4(10) + 3(20) + 4(50)$

Like terms can occur in any addition question. It doesn't have to be a monetary question. Any time you see two or more of the same number in an addition problem, they can be combined.

5 + 6 + 3 + 5 + 2 + 6 + 5	=	3(5) + 2(6) + 3 + 2
75 + 63 + 75 + 63 + 75	=	3(75) + 2(63)
5 + 5 + 5 + 5 + 5 + 4	=	5(5) + 4

Fractions

A fraction is simply a part of a whole thing. The example below is of a circle divided into four pieces. Each segment represents ¼ of the circle.

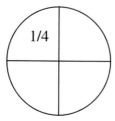

In each of the circles below, the same area is represented, but the area is divided into different numbers of equal parts.

1 / 2 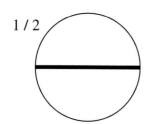   2 / 4 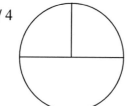   4 / 8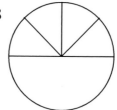

This diagram demonstrates that the fractions 1/2, 2/4 and 4/8 represent the same quantity.

1 / 3 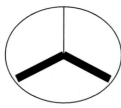   2 / 6    3 / 9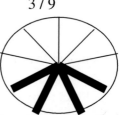

The fractions 1/3, 2/6 and 3/9 are equivalent. You can determine fractions of equivalent value by multiplying both the numerator and the denominator of the fraction by the same number.

$$\frac{1 \times 7}{3 \times 7} = \frac{7}{21} \qquad \text{thus} \qquad \frac{7}{21} = \frac{1}{3}$$

A similar rule holds when dividing the numerators and denominators of fractions. This is necessary to reduce fractions to their lowest form.

$$\frac{5 \text{ divided by } 5}{15 \text{ divided by } 5} = \frac{1}{3}$$

Improper Fractions

When a fraction has a larger numerator than denominator then the fraction is larger than one. The diagram below illustrates an example of improper fractions.

3 / 2   =   1 1/2

Adding and Subtracting Fractions

Whenever you are adding or subtracting fractions, you have to ensure that the denominators of the fractions are the same. For example:

$\frac{1}{2}$ + $\frac{6}{8}$ does not equal $\frac{7}{10}$

By multiplying both the denominator and the numerator of 1/2 by 4, you will be able to add the fractions together. 1 / 2 becomes 4 / 8.

$\frac{4}{8}$ + $\frac{6}{8}$ = $\frac{10}{8}$ = $\frac{5}{4}$

When you are adding and subtracting fractions, you also maintain the same denominator, and add or subtract the numerator.

$\frac{3}{4}$ - $\frac{1}{4}$ = $\frac{2}{4}$ = $\frac{1}{2}$ $\frac{3}{18}$ + $\frac{12}{18}$ = $\frac{15}{18}$ = $\frac{5}{6}$

$\frac{5}{10}$ - $\frac{3}{10}$ = $\frac{2}{10}$ = $\frac{1}{5}$ $\frac{7}{8}$ + $\frac{5}{8}$ = $\frac{12}{8}$ = $1 \frac{1}{2}$

Multiplying Fractions

When multiplying fractions, there is no need to find a common denominator. Simply multiply the two top numbers and then multiply the two bottom numbers. Multiplying two fractions together (other than improper) will result in a fraction that is smaller than the original numbers.

$\frac{4}{5}$ x $\frac{3}{4}$ = $\frac{12}{20}$ = $\frac{3}{5}$ $\frac{1}{2}$ x $\frac{1}{5}$ = $\frac{1}{10}$

$\frac{3}{4}$ x $\frac{7}{18}$ = $\frac{21}{72}$ = $\frac{7}{24}$ $\frac{3}{2}$ x $\frac{4}{5}$ = $\frac{12}{10}$ = $1 \frac{1}{5}$

Dividing Fractions

Division with fractions is very similar to multiplying with fractions.

12 divided by 12 = 1	12 goes into 12 once
12 divided by 6 = 2	6 goes into 12 twice
12 divided by 4 = 3	4 goes into 12 three times
12 divided by 3 = 4	3 goes into 12 four times
12 divided by 2 = 6	2 goes into 12 six times
12 divided by 1 = 12	1 goes into 12 twelve times
12 divided by 1/2 = 24	1/2 goes into 12 twenty four times

This is logical when you think about the statement on the right. Whenever you are dividing by a fraction you have to multiply one fraction by the reciprocal of the other. That is, when you divide one fraction by another, you have to multiply one fraction by the inverse of the other. For example:

$$\frac{1}{2} \div \frac{6}{7} = \frac{1}{2} \times \frac{7}{6} = \frac{7}{12}$$

$$\frac{3}{4} \div \frac{4}{5} = \frac{3}{4} \times \frac{5}{4} = \frac{15}{16}$$

$$1\frac{3}{4} \div \frac{4}{5} = \frac{7}{4} \times \frac{5}{4} = \frac{35}{16} = 2\frac{3}{16}$$

Whenever dividing mixed fractions (1 1/2, 2 3/4 etc) you must use improper fractions (3/2, 11/4 etc).

Percentages

It is important to have a solid background in decimals and fractions before you try to handle percentage questions. Percentages are simply fractions. Per means "out of" and cent means "a hundred". Percentages are fractions with 100 as a denominator. They are often noted with this sign: %.

10 % means 10 out of 100 or $\dfrac{10}{100}$

13 % means 13 out of 100 or $\dfrac{13}{100}$

100 % means 100 out of 100 or $\dfrac{100}{100}$

100% means everything. 100% of your salary is your whole salary. You simply follow the same rules of conversion from fractions to decimals for calculating percentages. Simply move the decimal points two places to the left to convert percents to decimals. This is essentially dividing the percentage by 100.

Example: 7 5 %   = 0 . 7 5

               8%   = 0 . 0 8

            5 3 . 5 % = 0 . 5 3 5

            2 0 8 %   = 2 . 0 8

Any percent larger than 100% indicates more than the whole. For example:

A man's stock portfolio is worth 125% of what it was a year ago. This means that the stocks are now worth 25% more. If his stocks were worth $500 last year, they would be worth:

$500 x 125% =
                         500
                     x 1.25
                      $ 625

Percentages with Fractions

Some questions you encounter may incorporate percentages and fractions. Examples include 2 1/2 % or 33 1/3 %. In order to deal with these problems, you must first convert the percentages to improper fractions.

$$2\ 1/2 = 5/2 \qquad\qquad 33\ 1/3 = 100/3$$

After this step you simply carry out the division question.

$$
\begin{array}{r}
2.5 \\
2\overline{)5.0} \\
4 \\
\overline{10} \\
10 \\
\overline{0}
\end{array}
\qquad
\begin{array}{r}
33.33 \\
3\overline{)100.00}
\end{array}
$$

Once you have the decimal equivalent of the percentage, you then follow the same rules that apply to a regular percentage. Divide the number by 100 or, more simply, move the decimal to the left twice. Thus:

$$2\ 1/2\% = 0.025 \qquad\qquad 33\ 1/3\% = 0.3333$$

Percentages You Should Memorize

25%	=	1 / 4	=	0.25
50%	=	1 / 2	=	0.5
75%	=	3 / 4	=	0.75
100%	=	4 / 4	=	1.00
33 1/3 %	=	1 / 3	=	0.333
66 2/3 %	=	2 / 3	=	0.666
10%	=	1 / 10	=	0.1
20%	=	1 / 5	=	0.2
40%	=	2 / 5	=	0.4
60%	=	3 / 5	=	0.6
80%	=	4 / 5	=	0.8

Decimal / Fraction Conversion Instruction

Fraction to Decimal

There are many situations where you will have to convert fractions to decimals. Decimals are often easier to work with. Changing fractions to decimals is simply a division problem. All you have to do is take the numerator and divide it by the denominator.

Examples:

$$1/2 = 2\overline{)1.0} \quad \frac{0.5}{}$$
$$-\underline{1.0}$$
$$0$$

$$4/5 = 5\overline{)4.0} \quad \frac{0.8}{}$$

$$1/3 = 3\overline{)1.000} \quad \frac{0.333}{}$$
$$-\underline{0.9}$$
$$0.10$$
$$-\underline{09}$$
$$010$$
$$-\underline{09}$$
$$1$$

Mixed Fractions

Mixed fractions have to first be converted to improper fractions before they can be converted to decimals. Multiplying the whole number by the denominator and adding the numerator will achieve this. As soon as the improper fraction is found, you calculate the decimal in the same way as above.

Example 1
$$3\frac{1}{2} = \frac{7}{2} \qquad 2\overline{)7.0} \quad \frac{3.5}{}$$

Multiply 3 by 2, and then add 1. This is the new numerator, and the denominator remains the same.

Example 2
$$2\frac{5}{6} = \frac{17}{6} \qquad 6\overline{)17.000} \quad \frac{2.833}{}$$

Decimal to Fraction

When converting decimals to fractions, place value is extremely important. The first decimal point to the right of the decimal point is the tenths, followed by the hundredths, thousandths, etc. All you have to do is properly line up the place value with the proper denominator.

$$0.1 \quad \text{is a way of writing} \quad \frac{1}{10}$$

$$0.01 \quad \text{is a way of writing} \quad \frac{1}{100}$$

and

$$0.6 \quad \text{is a way of writing} \quad \frac{6}{10}$$

$$0.78 \quad \text{is a way of writing} \quad \frac{78}{100}$$

There is one zero in the denominator for every place to the right of the period in the original decimal.

Exponents

Exponents indicate how many times a number should be multiplied by itself. If a number is raised to the power of 2, the number should be multiplied by itself twice. If the number is raised to the power of 6, the number should be multiplied by itself 6 times.

$$2^2 = 2 \times 2 = 4$$

$$2^3 = 2 \times 2 \times 2 = 8$$

$$2^4 = 2 \times 2 \times 2 \times 2 = 16$$

$$2^5 = 2 \times 2 \times 2 \times 2 \times 2 = 32$$

$$7^2 = 7 \times 7 = 49$$

$$5^4 = 5 \times 5 \times 5 \times 5 = 625$$

Positive and Negative Integers

You must have an understanding of positive and negative integers and how they react when they are added, subtracted, multiplied and divided by each other. Look at the number line below. Positive integers exist to the right of the zero and negative integers exist to the left of the zero.

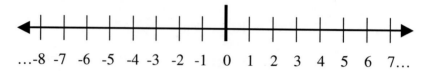

Adding Positive and Negative Integers

1) - 7 + 5 = -2   2) - 6 + 3 = -3
3) - 2 + 7 = 5   4) - 4 + 11 = 7

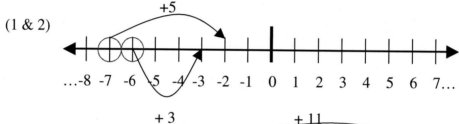

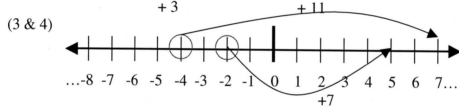

Subtracting Positive and Negative Integers

1) - 2 – 5 = -7   2) - 4 – 8 = -12
3) 4 – 7 = -3   4) 2 – 5 = -3

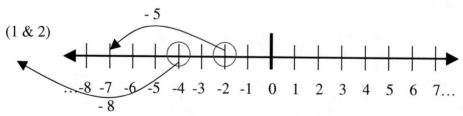

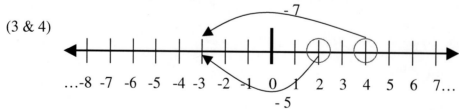

When adding and subtracting positive and negative integers you must know what to do when two signs are directly beside each other.

2 Positives	2 Negatives	Opposite Signs
+ + = +	- - = +	+ - = -

For instance:

$6 + (+3)$	$6 + (-3)$	$6 - (-3)$
$= 6 + 3$	$= 6 - 3$	$= 6 + 3$
$= 9$	$= 3$	$= 9$

Try these sample questions. The answers are below.

1) $5 - 9 =$ 2) $-4 + 6 =$ 3) $-5 - 2 =$ 4) $2 - 7 =$

5) $-2 + 5 =$ 6) $1 - 9 =$ 7) $4 - (+6) =$ 8) $-2 - (-4) =$

9) $+3 - (-6) =$ 10) $6 + (-4) =$ 11) $6 + (+2) =$ 12) $-3 + (-2) =$

Multiplying and Dividing Positive and Negative Integers

While multiplying and dividing positive and negative integers, remember the rules that apply to adding and subtracting integers with two signs directly beside each other.

2 Positives	2 Negatives	Opposite Signs
+ + = +	- - = +	+ - = -

You should break questions like this into two steps.

Step 1: Solve the equation ignoring the signs.

$6 \times (-3) = 18$	$-5 \times 4 = 20$
$5 \times (-7) = 35$	$-3 \times (-4) = 12$
$-12 \div (-4) = 3$	$-21 \div 3 = 7$
$36 \div (-9) = 4$	$-64 \div (-8) = 8$

If you ignored the + and − signs in front of the numbers you would end up with the answers above.

Step 2: Determine the + / - sign. The rules about + / - integers come into play. If there are two + signs, then the equation is positive. If there are two − signs, then the equation is also positive. If there is one + and one − sign, then the equation is negative.

$$6 \times (-3) = \textbf{-18} \ (+ / -) \qquad -5 \times 4 = \textbf{-20} \ (- / +)$$
$$5 \times (-7) = -\textbf{35} \ (- / +) \qquad -3 \times (-4) = \textbf{12} \ (- / -)$$
$$-12 \div (-4) = \textbf{3} \ (- / -) \qquad -21 \div 3 = -\textbf{7} \ (- / +)$$
$$36 \div (-9) = -\textbf{4} \ (+ / -) \qquad -64 \div (-8) = \textbf{8} \ (- / -)$$

The final answers are displayed in bold above.

Try these sample questions. The answers are posted below.

a) $3 \times (-6) =$ b) $-2 \times (-9) =$ c) $-18 \div (-9) =$

d) $7 \times 7 =$ e) $-72 \div 8 =$ f) $-12 \times (-9) =$

g) $7 \times (-6) =$ h) $-28 \div (-4) =$ i) $16 \div (-4) =$

j) $3 \times (-4) =$ k) $-45 \div (-15) =$ l) $-3 \times (2) =$

Answers to Sample Questions

1) $5 - 9 = \textbf{-4}$ 2) $-4 + 6 = \textbf{2}$ 3) $-5 - 2 = \textbf{-7}$

4) $2 - 7 = \textbf{-5}$ 5) $-2 + 5 = \textbf{3}$ 6) $1 - 9 = \textbf{-8}$

7) $4 - (+6) = \textbf{-2}$ 8) $-2 - (-4) = \textbf{2}$ 9) $+3 - (-6) = \textbf{9}$

10) $6 + (-4) = \textbf{2}$ 11) $6 + (+2) = \textbf{8}$ 12) $-3 + (-2) = \textbf{-5}$

---

a) $3 \times (-6) = \textbf{-18}$ b) $-2 \times (-9) = \textbf{18}$ c) $-18 \div (-9) = \textbf{2}$

d) $7 \times 7 = \textbf{49}$ e) $-72 \div 8 = \textbf{-9}$ f) $-12 \times (-9) = \textbf{108}$

g) $7 \times (-6) = \textbf{-42}$ h) $-28 \div (-4) = \textbf{7}$ i) $16 \div (-4) = \textbf{-4}$

j) $3 \times (-4) = \textbf{-12}$ k) $-45 \div (-15) = \textbf{3}$ l) $-3 \times (2) = \textbf{-6}$

Perimeters

Perimeter is defined as the border around an object, or the outside edge of an object.

Perimeter is calculated by adding the sides of the object together.

Perimeter = 6 + 5 + 5 + 5 + 5 + 6
= 32

Perimeter = 4 + 4 + 4 + 4
= 16

Perimeter = 3 + 3 + 4
= 10

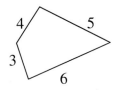

Perimeter = 3 + 4 + 5 + 6
= 18

Circumferences

Circumference is also defined as the border around a shape, but is always associated with a circle.

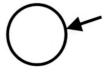

In order to determine the circumference of a circle, you must use a formula. You need to be familiar with some definitions.

$$\pi = 3.14 \text{ (pi)}$$

You are going to have to remember that pi is equal to 3.14.

Diameter (d)

Diameter is the distance from one edge of the circle, through the middle, to the opposite side of the circle.

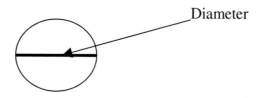

Radius (r)

Radius is defined as ½ of the diameter, or the distance from the mid-point of a circle to its outer edge.

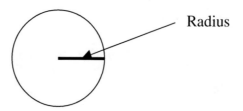

Formula for Calculating Circumference

$$C = 2 \text{ x } (\pi) \text{ x } r \qquad \text{or} \qquad C = d \text{ x } (\pi)$$

$$C = 2 \text{ x } (3.14) \text{ x } 5 \qquad\qquad C = 10 \text{ x } (3.14)$$

$$= 31.4 \text{ cm} \qquad\qquad\qquad = 31.4 \text{ cm}$$

The information you are given in a question will dictate the formula you should use to calculate the circumference. If you are given the radius, calculate the diameter by multiplying by two. Dividing the diameter by two will give you the radius.

Areas

Area is space that is occupied within the borders of a shape. It is measured in units squared and is represented by the area shaded in the shapes below.

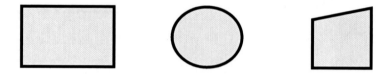

The three shapes you should know how to calculate area for are the triangle, rectangle and circle.

Area of a Rectangle or Square

To calculate the area of a square or rectangle, multiply the base of the object by its' height.

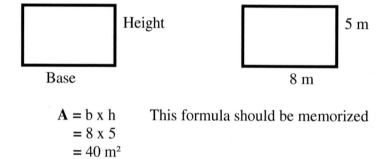

$A = b \times h$ This formula should be memorized
$\quad = 8 \times 5$
$\quad = 40 \text{ m}^2$

Area of a Triangle

To calculate the area of a triangle, follow the formula below.

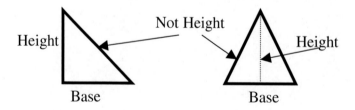

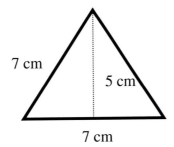

$A = \frac{1}{2} \times b \times h$ **This formula should be memorized.**
$= \frac{1}{2} \times 7 \times 5$
$= 17.5 \text{ cm}^2$

Remember that height is not necessarily an edge of the triangle, but the distance from the base to the top of the triangle.

Area of a Circle

To calculate the area of a circle, follow the formula below.

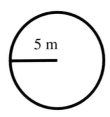

$A = \pi \, (\, r \,)^2$ **This formula should be memorized.**
$= (3.14)\,(5)^2$
$= (3.14)\,(25)$
$= 78.5 \text{ m}^2$

Other Shapes

You may have to calculate the area of shapes other than basic squares, triangles and circles. You can attempt to break shapes into smaller components and use the formulas above. For example:

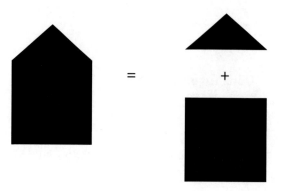

Calculate the area of the triangle and adding it to the area of the square results in the area of the whole shape.

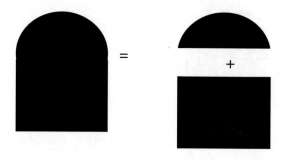

You can divide the shape on the left into a square and a half circle. Calculate the area of the square and the area of the circle. Divide the area of the circle in half and add the two together.

Volumes

Volume is defined as the area occupied by a three dimensional shape. If you pictured an empty cup, volume is the amount of liquid it contains. Calculating volume for different objects can be very difficult and involves complex formulas. We will discuss how to calculate the volume of three simple objects. Volume is always discussed in units cubed (example $3m^3$.)

Volume of a Cube

You should memorize the formula for calculating the volume of a cube.

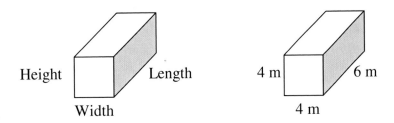

$$V = \text{length x width x height}$$
$$= 6 \times 4 \times 4$$
$$= 96 \text{ m}^3$$

Volume of a Cylinder

To calculate the volume of a cylinder, determine the area of the circle and multiply it by the height of the cylinder.

Radius = 5 m

Height = 10 m

$$V = \pi \, (r)^2 \text{ x height}$$
$$= (3.14) \, (5)^2 \, (10)$$
$$= 785 \text{ m}^3$$

Volume of a Triangular Shaped Object

To calculate the volume of an object like the one below, first calculate the area of the triangle and multiply it by the height of the object.

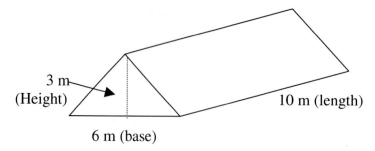

$$V = \tfrac{1}{2} \, (\text{base}) \, (\text{height}) \, (\text{length})$$
$$= \tfrac{1}{2} \, (6) \, (3) \, (10)$$
$$= 90 \text{ m}^3$$

Metric Conversions

The key to understanding metric conversions is to memorize the prefixes and roots to each word. The root of each word indicates the basic measurement (litre, metre, gram), while the prefixes determine the relative size of the measurement (larger or smaller units – milli, centi, kilo, etc,).

Prefixes

All units in the metric system are easily converted because they are all based on units of 10. When converting between different measurements of the same base unit, it is as easy as shifting the decimal point.

For example:

432,000 millimetres
43,200 centimetres   ALL EQUAL EACH OTHER
432 metres
0.432 kilometres

Length

Length is used to measure the distance between points. The base unit for length is the metre. The most common units you'll encounter with length include:

Millimetres – small units (25 millimetres in 1 inch)
Centimetres – small units (2.5 centimetres in 1 inch)
Metres – larger units (1 metre = 3.2 feet or 1.1 yards)
Kilometres – large units (1.6 kilometres in 1 mile)

Prefix	Example	Sign	Conversion
Milli	Millimetres	mm	1 m = 1000 mm
Centi	Centimetre	cm	1 m = 100 cm
Deci	Decimetre	dm	1 m = 10 dm
-	Metre	m	1 m = 1 m
Kilo	Kilometre	km	1 km = 1000 m

Volume

Volume is defined as the capacity of a given container. It usually measures the amount of liquid or gas that an object can hold. For example, the volume of a pop can is 355 millilitres, or the volume of a milk carton is 1 litre. The base unit for volume in the metric system is the litre. A litre is roughly the amount of milk that will fit into a milk carton or roughly three glasses of milk.

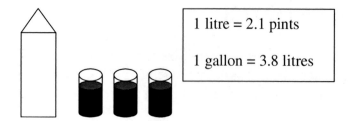

1 litre = 2.1 pints

1 gallon = 3.8 litres

The most common prefix used with volume is the millilitre (used to measure small amounts, such as tablespoons.) The majority of the time when measuring volume you will be using the litre measurement itself.

Prefix	Example	Sign	Conversion
Milli	Millilitres	mL	1 L = 1000 mL
Centi	Centilitres	cL	1 L = 100 cL
Deci	Decilitres	dL	1 L = 10 dL
-	Litres	L	1 L = 1 L
Kilo	Kilolitres	kL	1 kL = 1000 L

Mass or Weight

The base unit for weight in the metric system is the gram. The most common units you'll encounter with weight are:

Milligrams – very small (1000 milligrams in 1 gram)
Grams – small units (28.3 grams in 1 ounce)
Kilograms – large units (1 kilogram = 2.2 pounds)

Prefix	Example	Sign	Conversion
Milli	Milligrams	mg	1 g = 1000 mg
Centi	Centigram	cg	1 g = 100 cg
Deci	Decigram	dg	1 g = 10 dg
-	Gram	G	1 g = 1 g
Kilo	Kilogram	kg	1 kg = 1000 g

Algebraic Equations

Before beginning this section, make sure that you are comfortable with the rules of order of operation in mathematical equations. It is necessary to know in what order you add, subtract, divide and multiply in an equation.

Algebraic equations involve using letters and symbols to represent unknown numbers. In order to solve these equations you must isolate the unknown variable. We will begin with a couple of simple examples.

When solving algebraic equations, it is important to know the opposite mathematical operations. For example, subtraction is the opposite of addition and division is the opposite of multiplication. Square roots are the opposite of squaring. We will not cover square roots in this section.

$6 + y = 12$

$6 + y - \mathbf{6} = 12 - \mathbf{6}$

$y = 6$

> In order to isolate the "y", eliminate a + 6 on the left hand side of the equation. In algebraic equations, whatever you do to one side of the equation you must also do to the other side. Subtract 6 from both sides.

$y - 3 = 15$

$y - 3 + \mathbf{3} = 15 + \mathbf{3}$

$y = 18$

> In order to isolate the "y", eliminate a - 3 on the left hand side of the equation. Add 3 to both sides.

$7y = 42$

$7y / \mathbf{7} = 42 / \mathbf{7}$

$y = 6$

> In this case, "y" is multiplied by 7. To eliminate a number that is being multiplied, divide by the same number. Divide both sides by 7.

$y / 12 = 5$

$y / 12 \times \mathbf{12} = 5 \times \mathbf{12}$

$y = 60$

> In this case, "y" is divided by 12. To eliminate a number that is being divided, multiply by the same number. Multiply both sides by 12.

Practice solving some of these simple equations:

1) $y / 11 = 23$ 2) $15 + y = 63$ 3) $-5 + y = 10$

4) $13 (y) = 130$ 5) $5 y = 15$ 6) $6 + 3 + y = 56$

7) $2(y) = 56$ 8) $y / 8 = 4$ 9) $y (24) = 72$

Answers are below.

More Advanced Algebraic Equations

When solving equations, follow the order of operations which dictate that you perform equations within brackets, followed by exponents, then division and multiplication, and finally addition and subtraction. When isolating unknown variables, use the opposite order. We will not cover solving equations with exponents at this level.

$6 y + 12 = 84$

$6 y + 12 - \mathbf{12} = 84 - \mathbf{12}$

$6 y = 72$

$6 y / \mathbf{6} = 72 / \mathbf{6}$

$y = 12$

> In order to isolate the "y", first eliminate a + 12 on the left hand side of the equation. Subtract 12 from both sides. You are left with 6y = 12.
> To isolate "y", now simply divide both sides of the equation by 6.

$y / 3 + 12 - 2 = \mathbf{15 \ x \ 3} + 4$

$y / 3 + 12 - 2 = \mathbf{45} + \mathbf{4}$

$y / 3 + 12 - 2 = 49$

$y / 3 + 12 - 2 + \mathbf{2} = 49 + \mathbf{2}$

$y / 3 + 12 = 51$

$y / 3 + 12 - \mathbf{12} = 51 - \mathbf{12}$

$y / 3 = 39$

$y / 3 \ x \ \mathbf{3} = 39 \ x \ \mathbf{3}$

$y = 117$

> You may encounter equations where one side has operations without an unknown variable. In cases like this, solve the side without an unknown variable FOLLOWING THE STANDARD ORDER OF OPERATION RULES.
>
> After you have accomplished this, solve the equation in the standard manner. People more advanced in math will be able to consolidate portions of the left side as well, but unless you are comfortable you should proceed the way outlined to the left.

$(6 - y) \times 3 = 24$

$(6 - y) \times 3 / \mathbf{3} = 24 / \mathbf{3}$

$(6 - y) = 8$

$6 - y - \mathbf{6} = 8 - \mathbf{6}$

$- y = 2$

$- y \times \mathbf{(-1)} = 2 \times \mathbf{(-1)}$

$y = - 2$

Perform this equation following the standard rules. Leave the brackets until the end. When only the brackets remain, you can get rid of them as they no longer serve a purpose.

When you are left with an equation where the unknown is isolated, but negative, simply multiply both sides of the equation by – 1 to inverse the signs.

The end result is that y = - 2.

$18 / y = 2$

$18 / y \times \mathbf{(y)} = 2 \times \mathbf{(y)}$

$18 = 2 y$

$18 / \mathbf{2} = 2 y / \mathbf{2}$

$9 = y$

One other tricky situation you may encounter is when "y" appears on the bottom of a division equation. In order to solve for "y", move it from the bottom of the division sign by multiplying both sides of the equation by "y". The result is 18 = 2 y. Now solve the rest of the equation.

> WHATEVER YOU DO TO ONE SIDE OF AN EQUATION YOU MUST ALSO DO TO THE OTHER SIDE.

More Practice Questions

a) $3 (y) + 6 - 10 = 89$

b) $(y) / 6 + 24 - 2 = 14$

c) $- y (3) + 55 = 105$

d) $5 y - 32 = 24 (3)$

e) $-32 + 6y/2 = 64$

f) $22 y + 16 (8) = 6 y$

Answers:

1) 253	2) 48	3) 15
4) 10	5) 3	6) 47
7) 28	8) 32	9) 3

a) 31	b) - 48	c) –16.7
d) 20.8	e) 32	f) – 8

Teaching
Mechanical Aptitude

Below is a list of simple machines which firefighters often use to perform their duties.

- Lever
- Wheel and Axle
- Inclined Plane
- Belt Drive

- Pulley
- Screw
- Gears

Complex machines basically employ one or a combination of the above machines. The purpose of all these tools is to make given tasks easier. Mechanical movements and forces govern these tools.

Levers

Levers are devices we are familiar with as many of us grew up using them as toys such as teeter-totters. These tools allow lighter weights to lift heavier weights through the use of leverage. What you have to understand about levers is how the position of the fulcrum (pivot point) will affect different weights.

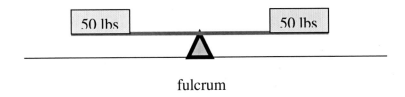

fulcrum

With two equal weights situated equidistant from the fulcrum, neither side should fall. The two weights will balance each other and neither side will go up or down.

If the same weights are not positioned equidistant from the fulcrum, the weight closer to the fulcrum will be lifted into the air by the weight further away.

As stated above, this is the principle of leverage. In order to lift the 50 lbs on the right, there wouldn't even need to be 50 lbs on the left. A lighter weight (amount of force) could lift the 50 lbs.

There is a mathematical equation which allows you to determine how much force is required to lift a weight depending on how far each weight is from the fulcrum.

Effort x Effort Distance = Resistance x Resistance Distance

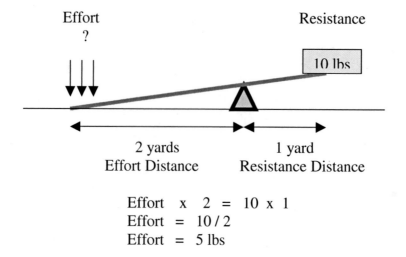

Effort
?

Resistance

10 lbs

2 yards
Effort Distance

1 yard
Resistance Distance

$$\text{Effort} \times 2 = 10 \times 1$$
$$\text{Effort} = 10 / 2$$
$$\text{Effort} = 5 \text{ lbs}$$

You should be aware of a second class of lever. Have you ever seen a situation such as this?

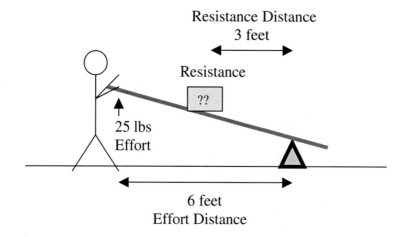

Resistance Distance
3 feet

Resistance

??

25 lbs
Effort

6 feet
Effort Distance

$$\text{Effort} \times \text{Distance Effort} = \text{Resistance} \times \text{Resistance Distance}$$

$$25 \times 6 = \text{Resistance} \times 3$$
$$\text{Resistance} = 150 / 3$$
$$\text{Resistance} = 50 \text{ lbs}$$

In this configuration, you can lift 50 lbs by using 25 lbs of effort.

General Rules of Levers

1) The closer the resistance is to the fulcrum the less effort is required to lift the object.

A

B

Lifting the box in example A requires more effort than lifting the box in example B. You should also notice that in example B the person loses potential height.

2) The further the effort is from the fulcrum the less effort is required to lift the object.

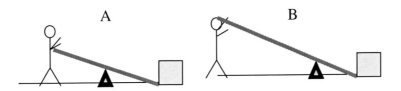

Lifting the box in example A requires more effort than lifting the box in example B. You should also notice that in example B the person is required to move the lever a greater distance to gain the mechanical advantage.

Pulleys

Firefighters often use pulleys in order to lift or pull heavy objects. They can be either fixed (motionless) or moveable. In order to work with pulleys, you need to understand the mechanical advantage (M.A.) they provide. To determine this, count the number of cables that are supporting the weight, excluding the cable which is acting as the Effort. Consider the examples below.

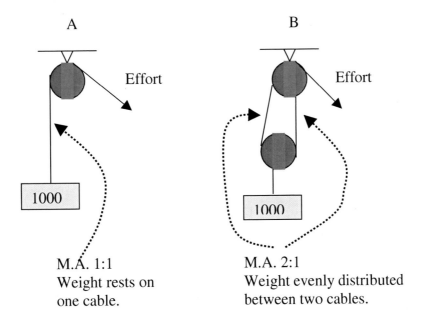

M.A. 1:1
Weight rests on
one cable.

M.A. 2:1
Weight evenly distributed
between two cables.

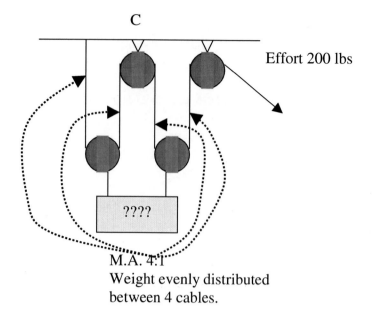

C

Effort 200 lbs

????

M.A. 4:1
Weight evenly distributed
between 4 cables.

The mathematical formula to calculate the Effort requirements is as follows:

$$\text{Effort} = \frac{\text{Weight (resistance)}}{\text{Mechanical Advantage}}$$

In Example A, the weight is 1000 lbs and the M.A. is 1. With this system, it would take 1000 lbs of effort to lift the 1000 lb weight.

$$\text{Effort} = 1000 / 1 = 1000 \text{ lbs}$$

In example B, the weight is 1000 lbs and the M.A. is 2. With this system, it would take 500 lbs of effort to lift the 1000 lb weight.

$$\text{Effort} = 1000 / 2 = 500 \text{ lbs}$$

In example C, the effort is 200 lbs and the M.A. is 4. With 200 lbs of effort you would be able to lift up to 800 lbs.

$$200 = \text{Weight} / 4$$

$$\text{Weight} = 200 \times 4 = 800 \text{ lbs}$$

As with levers, the Mechanical Advantage comes with a price. As Effort decreases with Mechanical Advantage, so does potential height. In other words, the more pulleys you use, the less high you can raise the object without pulling more rope through the system. There is a formula to determine the length of cable that is hauled through a pulley system and the height the object is actually raised.

$$\text{Length of Pull} = \text{Height (lift)} \times \text{Mechanical Advantage}$$

Wheel and Axle

One of the most recognized wheel and axle systems is a water well. This system involves a large wheel attached to a rod or axle or smaller wheel that performs work. When someone turns the large wheel handle at a well, this turns the smaller rod, which winds the rope to raise the bucket.

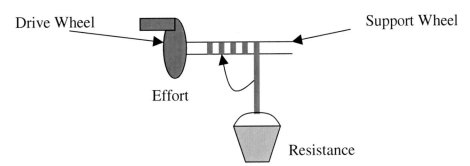

Drive Wheel   Support Wheel

Effort

Resistance

As with most mechanical devices, the wheel and axle makes the job of raising the water, or the resistance, easier. The larger the drive wheel is in relation to the support wheel, the less effort is required to lift the same resistance weight. You must know how to calculate the circumference in order to work with these problems. This is taught in the math teaching section, but here is a quick reminder of the formula:

$$C = 2(\pi)(r)$$
C = circumference
$\pi = 3.14$
r = radius

The formula for calculating the Mechanical Advantage of a wheel and axle is the following.

(Effort) x (C. Drive Wheel) = (Resistance) x (C. Support Wheel)

Effort = ???

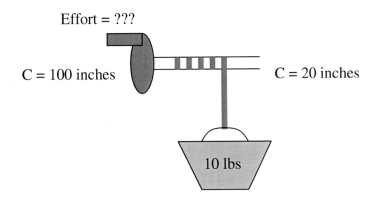

C = 100 inches   C = 20 inches

10 lbs

Effort x (C drive) = Resistance x (C support)
Effort x 100 = 10 x 20
Effort = 200 / 100
Effort = 2 lbs of effort would be required to lift the bucket

Screw

Screws are used for a variety of purposes, such as wedging into wood to hold material together, and also for lifting heavy objects such as motor vehicles through the use of a jackscrew. The composition of a screw is a rod with spiral threading on it.

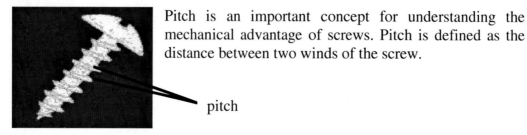

Pitch is an important concept for understanding the mechanical advantage of screws. Pitch is defined as the distance between two winds of the screw.

pitch

The pitch determines the amount of work that a screw performs during one complete revolution. The larger the pitch, the more work is done. However, larger pitches require more effort. Smaller pitches require more revolutions to complete the same job, but less effort is required to complete these revolutions.

As with the Wheel and Axle, you should be comfortable calculating circumference before attempting to solve problems with screws.

The mechanical advantage of a screw is calculated by dividing the circumference of the turning handle by the screw pitch.

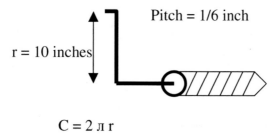

Pitch = 1/6 inch

r = 10 inches

$$C = 2 \pi r$$
$$= 2 (3.14) (10)$$
$$= 62.8 \text{ inches}$$

M.A. = Circumference of the handle ÷ Pitch of the Screw

M.A. = 62.8 ÷ 1/6

M.A. = 62.8 x 6

M.A. = 376.8 : 1

If you have difficulty remembering how to divide fractions, review the teaching material in the math section.

You have to multiply the number by the fraction's reciprocal.

The next step is to apply the mechanical advantage to a weight problem. Suppose you are required to lift a 3,000 lb motor vehicle. In using the jackscrew above, which has a M.A. of 377:1, how much effort would be required?

Effort = Resistance / Mechanical Advantage
Effort = 3,000 / 377
Effort = 8 lbs of effort would be required

Inclined Plane

An inclined plane is simply a ramp that is used to make lifting objects easier. They are used in a variety of situations, such as loading trucks to creating roads for trucks to drive out of open-pit mines. For an inclined plane, the effort required to lift an object decreases the longer the inclined plane is, and the shorter its height.

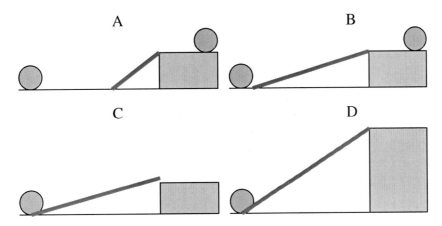

In order to move the drums above, option A would require more effort than option B, while option D would require more effort than option C.

There is a mathematical formula to calculate the amount of effort required to lift an object. The necessary variables are the height of the object, the weight of the object, and the length of the inclined plane.

Effort x Length of Plane = Resistance x Height

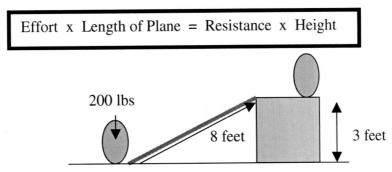

Effort x 8 = 200 x 3
Effort = 600 / 8
Effort = 75 lbs of effort is required to elevate the drum.

Gears and Belt Drives

Gears can be thought of as wheels with teeth which work together to change the direction of force. These wheels also increase or decrease the amount of torque (twisting force) that is applied from the drive gear (the gear that initiates the movement).

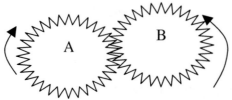

It is extremely important that you understand the dynamics of gears. When two gears intermesh teeth, Gear A (the drive gear) will spin the Gear B in the opposite direction regardless of whether this is clockwise or counterclockwise. If you want two gears to spin in the same direction, you need to have an intermediary gear between them.

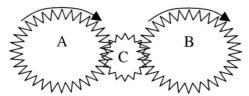

Gear C causes gear A and gear B to turn in the same direction.

In addition to changing the direction of force, gears can influence speed and torque if different sized gears are used with each other. Gear DG represents the drive gear, or the gear that is hooked up to a motor or another source of power.

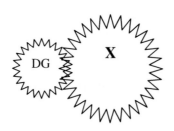

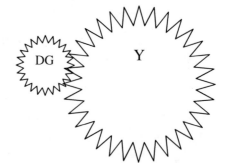

Gear X is twice as large as gear DG. Gear X will have twice as much torque, but will spin at ½ the speed.

Gear Y is three times the size of gear DG. Gear Y will have three times as much torque, but will spin at 1/3 the speed.

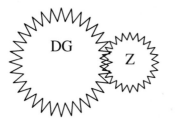

Gear Z is ½ the size of gear DG. Gear Z will have ½ as much torque, but will spin twice as fast as gear DG.

You should also be aware of other principles regarding different sized gears. If two gears of the exact same size are linked by a smaller (or larger) gear, there will be no difference in the speed or torque of the two gears being linked.

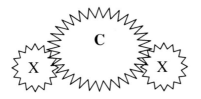

Both gear Y's will have the same speed and torque.

Both gear X's will have the same speed and torque.

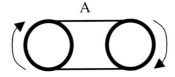

Belt Drives

Belt drives operate similarly to gears but are interconnected with a belt as opposed to intermeshing teeth. This configuration is frequently used in motor vehicles. One of the main differences in the operation of belt drives in comparison to the operation of gears is the fact that joined belt drives spin in the same direction unless the belt between the two wheels is twisted.

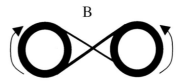

In example A, both wheels will spin in the same direction. In example B, the twist in the belt causes the wheels to spin in opposite directions.

Belt drives follow the same principles as gears in regards to torque and speed for differing wheel sizes.

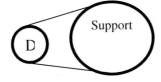

Wheel A is the drive gear and is ½ the size of the support wheel. The support wheel will therefore have twice as much torque, but will only spin at ½ the speed.

Teaching Material General

TOOLS

Hammers

Hammers are instruments used for pounding. For the most part they serve the purpose of driving nails into material, breaking objects apart, or driving other tools into material. Become familiar with the following types of hammers.

	Ball Peen Hammer Hammer used in metal work such as forging or rivet setting.
	Claw Hammer General hammer used in carpentry to both drive and extract nails.
	Rubber Mallet Drives materials without causing damage to the finish of a work piece or the tools involved.
	Sledge Hammer Heavy-duty instrument primarily used for breaking concrete, driving posts, etc. There are various sizes with different weighted heads.

Measuring Devices

Below is an extensive list of measuring devices. They include instruments used to measure an objects length, level, level of currents or angles.

	Carpenter's Steel Square Used to check right angles during framing to ensure square shapes. Contains measuring gradations.
	Combination Square Can serve as a try square, mitre square and level. Contains measuring gradations.
	Compass Inscribes circles or arcs and can be used to calibrate equal divisions on a line.

	Inside Calipers Transfers internal measurements to a ruler for precise measurements. Can also match two different items to determine a fit.
	Outside Calipers Can be used to transfer external measurements to rulers. Also capable of matching two items to compare fit.
	Micrometre Calipers Used for precise measurements ranging from 0 to 300 millimetres or 0 to 12 inches.
	Slide Calipers Similar to vernier callipers, but are not as accurate. Measuring gradations are larger with a measuring capacity up to 3 inches or 8 cm.
	Vernier Calipers Used for precise internal or external measurements. More precise than slide callipers but for larger measurements than micrometer callipers. (150 to 1800 mm or 6 to 72 inches).
	Level Measures the accuracy of level surfaces and true horizontal lines.
	Plumb Bob Used to determine a vertical line.
	Steel Ruler Measurement device with linear gradations, which can also be used as a straightedge.

	T – Bevel Marks or verifies angles on material. Often used with a protractor, which serves as a reference point.
	Tape Measure Measuring device with flexible metal tape that has measuring gradations.
	Wind Up Tape Measure Measuring device with gradations on a metallic tape. Small crank on the side is used to wind up the tape.
	Tire Gauge Used to measure the pressure of tires by attaching the end of the spout to ensure proper inflation
	Triangle Used to draw angles, and measure the accuracy on materials.
	Try Square Used to determine whether or not a work piece is square.
	Voltmetre / Ammeter / Ohmeter Unit used to measure the flow of electricity through a conductor (volt), the amount of electrical current flow (amm) or the resistance in a given unit or circuit (ohm).

Pliers

Pliers are most often used for gripping small objects to assist in manipulating them. One of the most common uses is forming shapes in wires.

	End-Cutting Pliers Crops metal wire close to a work surface.
	Needle-Nose Pliers Cuts and shapes thin-strand wire. Can grip small items in areas lacking space.
	Side Cutting Pliers Effective for cutting metal wire.

	Slip Joint Pliers
	Used to grip items with a pivot which allows two different jaw settings.

Saws

Saws are generally used for cutting material. It is important to understand that different saws are more suitable for different materials and different types of cuts. Different blades have to be used if you are cutting across the grain of wood (cross cutting) or cutting along the grain of the wood (ripping).

	Chain Saw Used in the cutting down of trees and cutting logs to specific lengths.
	Circular Saw Uses a variety of blades in order to cut lumber, certain metals, concrete or plywood to various sizes.
	Compass Saw Cuts holes in panels. Because this saw does not have a frame, it is not restricted to an edge of a work piece like a coping or hack saw.
	Coping Saw Effective for making curved cuts in a variety of materials.
	Hack Saw Cuts through metal sheets, piping, plastics, etc.
	Hand Saw Cuts through wood boards, sheets, or panels to various sizes. Can crosscut (across the grain) or rip (cut with the grain) or a combination depending on the teeth.
	Reciprocating Saw Power saw used much the same way as a handsaw or compass saw. Effective with wood, plastics, or thin metals. Various blades can be used depending on requirements.

	Saber Saw
	Effective for cutting curves in materials depending on blade selection.
	Table Saw Used to cut boards of various length. Depending on the blade can be used for crosscutting or ripping.

Screwdrivers

Screwdrivers are most often used to drive screws into material in order to fasten objects together. Different screw-heads require different drivers.

	Allen Key L-shaped hexagonal key used to tighten or loosen setscrews.
	Jeweler's Screwdrivers Used with small screws such as found in eyeglass hinges, wrist watches and electrical equipment. Drives and loosens screws.
	Phillips Screwdriver Used to drive Phillips head screws (cross).
	Robertson Screwdrivers Used to drive Robertson-head screws. More prominent in Canada than the United States.
	Slotted (conventional) Screwdrivers Used to drive slotted head screws.

Wrenches

Wrenches are most often defined as tools for turning nuts, bolts or pipes. There are several different types of wrenches, which have different uses, different strengths and different drawbacks.

	Bolts Used with nuts to hold two separate parts together.
	Box Wrench Used to tighten or loosen nuts and bolts. Allows more torque than an open wrench, but takes longer to use due to constant refitting on the bolt.
	Channel Locks Used like traditional pliers, with the ability to adjust jaw length to accommodate larger stock.
	Crescent Wrench An adjustable wrench. Tightens and loosens nuts and bolts of various sizes.
	Open-ended Wrench Tightens and loosens nuts and bolts. More useful than box wrenches in areas where there are obstructions above nuts.
	Pipe Wrench Grips round objects such as pipes and steel rods. The wrench is adjustable to accommodate various sizes.
	Ratchet Very common tool for tightening or loosening bolts. Eliminates the need to readjust for another grip as with most wrenches.
	Strap Wrench Used specifically to remove or tighten oil filters. Usually found in an automotive repair shop.

Carpentry Tools

The tools listed below are most often used with woodwork but may have applications beyond woodwork.

	Awl Starts holes in wood to allow nails and screws to follow.
	Belt Sander Sands wood, steel or plastic. The sheets run through the machine which are embedded with various abrasives. Back and forth motion is used.
	Bench Grinder Used to sharpen tools and remove rough edges. Can act as a buffer to clean and polish metal work if a wire brush is attached.
	Brace Manually drills holes through wood or provides additional torque in driving screws.
	C-Clamp Clamps wood or metal for various purposes.
	Centre Punch Marks and guides the placement of drill points.
	Drill Bits Used in power drills or braces for drilling holes. Various bits include the spade bit, auger bit, turn screw bit and ream.
	Drill Press Stationary power drill which can be used for drilling holes of various sizes depending on the bit.
	Electric Router Cuts grooves and mouldings of various shapes and sizes. Different types include dovetail, rabbit, etc.;

	Files Several different types used to file surfaces of most materials. Flat files, triangular files (angles or square corners) and round files (smooth or round openings) are all examples.
	Finishing Sander Uses light abrasive paper. Mechanism relies on vibration.
	Jack Plane Smoothes a wooden work piece.
	Parallel Clamps Used to secure boards or framing while they are being glued. Able to secure an angled object unlike pipe clamps.
	Power Drill Used to drive screws into material, or with bits to drill holes of various sizes. Can also have sanding disks, buths or lathes applied. Very flexible and fast tool.
	Vice Used to hold or secure a wood or metal work piece while work is being performed on it.
	Whetstone Tool used to primarily sharpen tools. A stone comprised of a gritty abrasive.
	Wood Chisel Coming in a variety of shapes and sizes, wood chisels are primarily used to trim or groove wood. Often used with some form of hammer.

Electrical Tools

Below is a small list of tools that are commonly used by electricians.

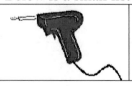	**Soldering Gun** Used in electrical work to solder wire to form contact terminals.

	Soldering Iron
	Heats metal and solder to form joints.
	Utility Knife
	General-purpose knife, often called an exacto knife.
	Wire Strippers
	Used similar to a pair of pliers to cut and strip insulation from wire. Can also be used to crimp terminals.

Metal Working Tools

Below is a small list of tools that are commonly used by metal workers.

	Arc Welder
	Uses electrical current to fuse pieces of metal together (rated in amperage).
	Bolt Cutters
	Cuts through steel rods, bolts, and locks. Employs the use of compound levers.
	Cold Chisel
	Flat chisel used to chip or cut cold metal including bolts and chain links.
	Multi-Purpose Tool
	Serves several functions including pliers, screwdrivers, knife and file.
	Pipe Cutter
	Cuts metal pipe by continually circling the pipe and increasing the torque.
	Propane Torch
	Heat source that has the ability to braze and solder pipe work. Heat can also be effective for loosening tight nuts and bolts.

	**Snips** Used to cut through sheet metal.

Miscellaneous Tools

The tools listed below can fall into several categories. You should be familiar with all of their uses.

	Axe Cutting tool used to chop trees down or hewing of wood.
	Pick Axe Breaks up hard material such as concrete, asphalt, etc. Can be used to pierce through walls in fire situations.
	Brick Trowel Used while working with bricks or concrete. Shapes, spreads and smoothes mortar.
	Broom Used to sweep up debris.
	Caulking Gun Applies sealants to joints such as window frames, doors, roofing vents or floor tiles.
	Crow Bar / Wrecking Bar Used to pry things apart, remove nails. Acts as a lever
	Glass Cutter Used to cut holes through glass surfaces.
	Hatchet Used to trim wood and can also be used as a hammer.

	Lopping Shears Gardening tool used for pruning tree branches and shrubs.
	Plunger Creates back pressure on obstructions to clear debris blocking drains.
	Rake Used to collect debris.
	Shovel Various uses including lifting debris or sprinkling earth or other materials.
	Skimmer Float While working with either wet plaster or concrete it can smooth the material to create a clean finish.
	Trowel Used to dig into earth or in the case of a mason's trowel to smooth and shape mortar when working with bricks or concrete.

Judgment Section

Framework for Analysis

It is important to have a framework for how you will approach judgment questions during an examination process. You must know how to establish hierarchies in order to prioritize activities and handle conflicting job requirements. Below is a possible value hierarchy that can be used to resolve difficult decisions.

1) Protection of Life and Limb.
This is a firefighter's first priority and supersedes all other decisions. This includes the lives of fellow firefighters as well.

2) Obeying Orders in Emergency Situations
Firefighters have to be able to follow instructions even though they may not fully understand the justification for them.

3) Protection of Property
This is a primary duty of firefighters.

4) Performing Other Required Duties
Some of the many other duties of lesser priority which firefighters have to perform include training, maintenance and public events.

Emergency Response Priorities

Fire departments will train you to effectively manage emergency scenes by working through a list of priorities. Here is a general framework of operations you should be considering while responding to emergency calls.

1) Create a Safe Work Area	There is no point tending to any of the following steps if you are going to be killed or seriously injured. If you are in serious danger, either get to a safe area or do something to address that danger. Creating this safe area includes getting victims who are in immediate danger to safety as well.
2) Call for any needed assistance	This sometimes has to occur as Step 1. If you act before calling for help, or if something happens to you, help may not arrive. Calling for proper assistance is extremely important. Possible providers of assistance could include fire personnel, police, ambulance, or other parties such as tow truck operators.

3) Treat life threatening injuries	You should always prioritize medical assistance to those that need it the most. While you are treating individuals you should prioritize ailments as your CPR and First Aid training dictates. Treat the most serious threats first.
4) Treat other injuries	As the emergency situation is brought under control (Step 1) and serious injuries are tended to, the next step is to provide medical treatment and transport of the injured to hospitals as required.
5) Restore order, assist police	After the primary concerns of eliminating the danger and treating the injured have been accomplished, firefighters should then assist in restoring order to the scene by helping other agencies such as the police in whatever way they can.

First Aid and CPR Minor Review

Before applying to the fire department you should be up-to-date in your First Aid and CPR training. Things you should be aware of include treating collapses and non-responsive victims. The A, B, C's of CPR are outlined below.

1) Airway
Ensure the airway is unobstructed.

2) Breathing
Check to see if the victim is breathing.

3) Circulation
Check to see that the blood is flowing (pulse)

After these priorities are taken care of you should then check for any other medical concerns the victim may have, including broken bones, injured spine, shock, etc.

Interpersonal Relations

As a firefighter you will be working in a team environment. You will have to count on your co-workers in life and death situations, and they will have to count on you. Respect is essential among firefighters. It must be maintained between firefighters of different ranks and between firefighters with different levels of knowledge and experience.

Concern for Safety

Respect for Chain of Command

Concern for Fellow Firefighters

Personal Accountability

The types of questions outlined below are subjective and often difficult to answer. Make sure you review the answer explanations after you have completed the test.

Fire Extinguishers Classes

Class A – Primarily used on materials such as paper, wood, and cloth which are combustible. Typically water or dry chemical filled.
Class B – Primarily used on gases or petroleum products such as propane, or gasoline.
Class C – Used on the same materials as Class A and Class B, but can also be used on fires involving electric current as the extinguishing agent is nonconductive. You should shut off the power before confronting an electrical fire.
Class D – Used on materials such as combustible metals and extremely volatile solids including magnesium, potassium and sodium. Special extinguishing agents are required to put out fires in this class.

Fires and fire extinguishers tend to fall into two or more classes. It is important to have a versatile extinguisher that can handle multiple classes of fires. If an extinguisher is rated A, B, C you can use it on combustible materials, gases, liquids, and petroleum products even if there is the threat of an electric current. If the extinguisher was only labeled A, B and you attempted to use it with an electrical fire, you could be injured. Know the types of extinguishers that exist, and know the conditions that are present when you attempt to put out a fire.

Performance Capability Questions

You will be asked to rate how well you would be able to carry on your professional duties based on some of the traumatic events you will be exposed to as a firefighter. As with the Distraught Response Questions, no one answer will cause you to fail the exam. However, problems may arise with your pattern of answer choices.

As a firefighter you will have to continue performing your duties no matter how distraught the situation makes you. If you continually answer questions of this nature by stating you would be unable to continue performing your duties, you will not pass this examination. Answers should be weighted towards being able to perform your duties. There is little use in hiring someone to be a firefighter if they are incapable of performing the necessary tasks. If you found yourself answering these types of questions with low rankings, or towards the middle, firefighting may not be the career for you. If you answered the questions with certainty and confidence (7 – 9) then you are in good shape to proceed.

Confidence Analysis

You will be asked to evaluate your confidence in decisions you might have to make during emergency situations. In this type of exam, answer patterns are far more important than individual answers.

Think about these questions logically. You will be asked to make a decision and then be asked how you feel about your decision. If you answer that you aren't confident about the decision, then you are admitting that you guessed at the answer. That means that if you got the above answer correct, it was by luck, not by knowledge.

Another assumption that can be inferred if you answer these questions with little confidence is that you are indecisive and incapable of standing behind your choice of direction.

All of your answer choices should demonstrate a high degree of confidence in your decision. If you come across one or two questions for which you really did not know the answer, and so guessed at it, then answering without confidence is acceptable. This will demonstrate your honesty. However, the vast majority of the answers however should demonstrate confidence.

Distraught Response Questions

During your testing you will be questioned on how you would feel while dealing with various emergency situations. You will be asked to rate your response, and you will be judged on the consistency of your answers. All of the questions relate to a similar experience, and should have been scored by you with similar answers.

- Dealing with death
- Dealing with minor injuries
- Dealing with major injuries
- Dealing with drowning
- Dealing with being unable to rescue a victim

Your specific answers aren't important, but your pattern of response is. For example, if you answered the questions below the following way there may be a problem with your truthfulness.

1) Seeing a dead elderly man.	3	**7**
2) Seeing a dead teenage girl.	5	**8**
3) Seeing a dead 40-year-old husband.	8	**8**
4) Seeing a dead baby.	9	**9**

The answers are not consistent. If you found your answers vary by three or more numbers, then you may not pass the actual test. The numbers in bold to the right would be a more appropriate response. All of these answers are very closely rated. Once again, we stress that the particular answer is less important than your pattern of choices.

There will be too many of these types of questions to memorize in a testing environment. The best option is to think about whatever the situation is and ANSWER THE QUESTIONS HONESTLY.

PRACTICE EXAMS

The CPS practice tests contain five sections. Start with Section 1 – Memory – and work your way through the remaining sections (Comprehension, Work Relations, Mechanical Reasoning and Arithmetic Reasoning).

The Memory questions are based on the passage on page 99. Have a friend read the passage to you once from start to finish at a normal pace without repeating any portions. For the Memory component, you are not permitted to take any notes.

The only materials you can use during the test are a pencil and scrap paper. No calculators, books or counting devices are permitted. After the memory passage has been read, give yourself ninety minutes to complete the exam.

Answer Sheet Practice Test 1 to Prepare for the CPS Tests

Memory	Reading Comp	Work Relations
A B C D	A B C D	A B C D
1) ○ ○ ○ ○	21) ○ ○ ○ ○	41) ○ ○ ○ ○
2) ○ ○ ○ ○	22) ○ ○ ○ ○	42) ○ ○ ○ ○
3) ○ ○ ○ ○	23) ○ ○ ○ ○	43) ○ ○ ○ ○
4) ○ ○ ○ ○	24) ○ ○ ○ ○	44) ○ ○ ○ ○
5) ○ ○ ○ ○	25) ○ ○ ○ ○	45) ○ ○ ○ ○
6) ○ ○ ○ ○	26) ○ ○ ○ ○	46) ○ ○ ○ ○
7) ○ ○ ○ ○	27) ○ ○ ○ ○	47) ○ ○ ○ ○
8) ○ ○ ○ ○	28) ○ ○ ○ ○	48) ○ ○ ○ ○
9) ○ ○ ○ ○	29) ○ ○ ○ ○	49) ○ ○ ○ ○
10) ○ ○ ○ ○ ___/ 20	30) ○ ○ ○ ○ ___/ 20	50) ○ ○ ○ ○ ___/ 20
11) ○ ○ ○ ○	31) ○ ○ ○ ○	51) ○ ○ ○ ○
12) ○ ○ ○ ○	32) ○ ○ ○ ○	52) ○ ○ ○ ○
13) ○ ○ ○ ○	33) ○ ○ ○ ○	53) ○ ○ ○ ○
14) ○ ○ ○ ○	34) ○ ○ ○ ○	54) ○ ○ ○ ○
15) ○ ○ ○ ○	35) ○ ○ ○ ○	55) ○ ○ ○ ○
16) ○ ○ ○ ○	36) ○ ○ ○ ○	56) ○ ○ ○ ○
17) ○ ○ ○ ○	37) ○ ○ ○ ○	57) ○ ○ ○ ○
18) ○ ○ ○ ○	38) ○ ○ ○ ○	58) ○ ○ ○ ○
19) ○ ○ ○ ○	39) ○ ○ ○ ○	59) ○ ○ ○ ○
20) ○ ○ ○ ○	40) ○ ○ ○ ○	60) ○ ○ ○ ○

Mech. Aptitude	Mathematics
A B C D	A B C D
61) ○ ○ ○ ○	81) ○ ○ ○ ○
62) ○ ○ ○ ○	82) ○ ○ ○ ○
63) ○ ○ ○ ○	83) ○ ○ ○ ○
64) ○ ○ ○ ○	84) ○ ○ ○ ○
65) ○ ○ ○ ○	85) ○ ○ ○ ○
66) ○ ○ ○ ○	86) ○ ○ ○ ○
67) ○ ○ ○ ○	87) ○ ○ ○ ○
68) ○ ○ ○ ○	88) ○ ○ ○ ○
69) ○ ○ ○ ○	89) ○ ○ ○ ○
70) ○ ○ ○ ○ ___/ 20	90) ○ ○ ○ ○ ___/ 20
71) ○ ○ ○ ○	91) ○ ○ ○ ○
72) ○ ○ ○ ○	92) ○ ○ ○ ○
73) ○ ○ ○ ○	93) ○ ○ ○ ○
74) ○ ○ ○ ○	94) ○ ○ ○ ○
75) ○ ○ ○ ○	95) ○ ○ ○ ○
76) ○ ○ ○ ○	96) ○ ○ ○ ○
77) ○ ○ ○ ○	97) ○ ○ ○ ○
78) ○ ○ ○ ○	98) ○ ○ ○ ○
79) ○ ○ ○ ○	99) ○ ○ ○ ○
80) ○ ○ ○ ○	100) ○ ○ ○ ○

It is Sunday the 25th of August. You are assigned to Firehall #6, which is located at the intersection of Yorkville and Bloor Streets. You are assigned to Pumper #6 as the driver. Your wife, Sandra, said goodbye to you this morning but your two children, John and Shelley, didn't notice you leave for work because they were still sleeping. The day shift starts at 6:00 am. This means you usually leave the house at 5:30 am in order to get there in time to relieve the night shift by about 5:45 am.

When you arrive at the hall you are told that there are 4 others working with you on the pumper that day: Andy, Ben, Chris and Danny. Ben is the captain of the truck and your immediate supervisor. This is outlined to you at the morning meeting, which began at 6:30 am today.

The day starts off slowly. After finishing cleaning duties on the trucks, you enjoy some downtime. Later, you catch up on some readings that you have to get through for promotional exams coming up in the near future.

At 11:30 am the alarm goes off and you are dispatched to attend 125 Walmer Avenue for a house on fire. Neighbours have reported that there are flames visible from the second story windows at the back of the house. The aerial truck has also been dispatched and will pull out right behind you. A pumper from neighbouring Firehall #5 has also been dispatched, as well as a hazardous material unit and the district chief.

You proceed to the truck with your co-workers. After quickly dressing and getting your gear in order you hop into the driver seat with your captain, Ben, beside you. You hit the lights and sirens and pull out from the hall. You drive down Yonge Street and cut across Glenville Road, which takes you to Walmer Avenue. You make a left onto Walmer Avenue and pull in front of 125 Walmer Avenue at 11:34 am. The actual fire is located across the street at 124 Walmer Avenue.

There are 2 children standing across the street. One child is wearing a blue cap, a black shirt and blue pants and appears to be 6-years-old. The other child is wearing a white top and green track pants and appears to be about the same age. As you pull up you can see heavy smoke escaping from the second floor windows at the front of the house.

There is a woman standing out front of the house. She yells that her name is Mary and that she is the owner of the house. Mary appears to be about 42-years-old and has on a green shirt and black pants. She is holding a portable telephone. She keeps screaming that she has four children and can only find two of them. Kevin and Sean are across the street where it's safe, but she can't find Jamie or Jane.

Jane is 5-years-old, Kevin is 7, Sean is 12 and Jamie is 13. Jamie has blonde hair and blue eyes. Jane has shoulder length brown hair and was wearing blue coveralls and a white shirt. Their rooms are on the second floor in the front of the house. There are two staircases in the house. One is located in the front hall and the second is in kitchen at the rear of the house.

As you survey the area you see a fire hydrant out front of 129 Walmer Avenue. Andy begins setting up the hose for water pressure. As the hoses become charged you are ordered by Ben to enter the house with Chris and the line. The second pumper arrives on the scene at 11:38 am. The aerial pulled up on scene at the same time you did.

A search of the house reveals an active fire in the back two bedrooms at the top of the staircase accessible from the kitchen. Chris finds Jamie unconscious in the front bedroom and the two of you rush the child outside. You notice three firefighters from the second pumper enter the burning building as you leave it. One of them states that Jane has been found in the backyard and that she is safe. Jamie is laid out on the front lawn a safe distance from the fire. He has no vital signs.

You and Andy begin emergency CPR on the unresponsive child. Your captain contacts dispatch in order to call for an ambulance. The ambulance arrives at 11:55 am – exactly 5 minutes after your captain put in the call.

Paramedics take over CPR and life saving efforts on the child. They are successful and the child begins to breathe on his own and has a regular heartbeat. Jamie is rushed to Mount Sinai Hospital for further treatment and observation.

The fire is brought under control and put out at 12:15 pm. There is a total of $100,000 damage to the house and its contents. Jamie's condition is updated to stable and a full recovery is expected. Other than that, there are no injuries in the event.

MEMORY COMPONENT

Question 1

On which date did the passage occur?

a) Sunday, August 1

b) Tuesday, August 25

c) Sunday, August 25

d) Saturday, August 29

Question 2

Who are your co-workers on the pumper?

a) Jamie, Sean, Ben, Andy

b) Danny, Ben, Chris, Andy

c) Jane, Kevin, Jason, Andy

d) Andy, Ben, Chris, David

Question 3

Where were you assigned to work?

a) Firehall # 6

b) Firehall # 8

c) Firehall # 5

d) none of these

Question 4

What time does the dayshift begin at your Firehall?

a) 5:30 am

b) 5:45 am

c) 6:00 am

d) 6:30 am

Question 5

Who is your immediate supervisor?

a) Andy

b) Chris

c) Danny

d) Ben

Question 6

What truck were you assigned to?

a) Pumper #6

b) Pumper #5

c) Pumper #4

d) Pumper #7

Question 7

What other truck is located at your station?

a) Another pumper

b) Hazardous Material Unit

c) An aerial tower

d) An aerial

Question 8

What time did the alarm go off?

a) 11:30 am

b) 11:35 am

c) 11:20 am

c) 11:15 am

Question 9

What was reported to you at the station?

a) Visible flames from the main floor windows

b) Smoke escaping from front windows of second floor

c) Visible flames from front windows of second floor

d) Visible flames from second floor rear windows

Question 10

Where was the fire located when you arrived on scene?

a) 122 Walmer Avenue   b) 123 Walmer Avenue

c) 124 Walmer Avenue   d) 125 Walmer Avenue

Question 11

What do you notice about the house as you pull up out front of it?

a) Visible flames from the second floor windows

b) Heavy smoke escaping from the second floor windows

c) 4 children standing across the street

d) 3 children standing across the street

Question 12

What are the names of the missing children who may still be in the building when you arrive on scene?

a) Kevin and Sean   b) Sean and Jane

c) Jane and Jamie   d) Jamie and Kevin

Question 13

What are Jamie's physical characteristics?

a) Blonde hair, green eyes   b) Brown hair blue eyes

c) Brown hair, blue eyes   d) Blonde hair, blue eyes

Question 14

Where are the bedrooms of the two missing children?

a) In the front of the house on the third floor

b) In the front of the house on the second floor

c) In the rear of the house on the second floor

d) In the rear of the house on the third floor

Question 15

Where is there a staircase in the house?

a) Front Hall   b) Rear Hall

c) Kitchen   d) Both A & C

Question 16

Who entered the burning building with you to look for the two children?

a) Ben   b) Chris

c) Andy   d) Danny

Question 17

How many fire fighters from the other pumper entered the building as you were leaving it?

a) 3   b) 4

c) 5   d) 2

Question 18

Which child was still in the house after you and your partner left the house with the victim?

a) Jane   b) Jamie

c) Kevin   d) none of the above

Question 19

What hospital was the victim sent to?

a) Sick Children's Hospital   b) Mount Pleasant Hospital

c) Mount Sinai Hospital   d) Mount Saint Anne Hospital

Question 20

What time was the fire brought under control?

a) 12:00 pm   b) 12:10 pm

c) 12:15 pm   d) 12:30 pm

READING COMPREHENSION
Answer Questions 21 - 25 based on the following passage.

Two young boys and a young girl died yesterday when a fire broke out and destroyed their Montreal home. Police and fire department officials are still trying to determine the cause of the 5:50 a.m. fire that also killed the children's dog. Because of the scale of the fire and the loss of life, the police say they are treating the blaze as suspicious until a cause can be determined.

Firefighters found Jarmin and Kaylin Achria, ages 6 and 4, in a bedroom on the second floor of the three-storey townhouse. They were pronounced dead on arrival at hospital. Their 13-year-old sister, Jaya, who police said was babysitting the boys, was taken to Ottawa Specialty Burn Unit in critical condition. She died at about 1 p.m.

A fourth sibling, Dinesh, 12, escaped by climbing from a second-storey window onto the roof. Neighbours rescued him with a ladder and he was listed in good condition in hospital last night. At the time of the fire, their mother, Shayna Achria, was at Hotel Dieu Hospital in Montreal where she works as a radiologist.

According to firefighters, the fire originated in the basement of the Balsam Avenue home, which is part of the Parkville Housing Co-operative. "The heat and smoke were intense. We could see it from at least 6 blocks away," said platoon chief James Jessop. "There was almost nothing left of the ground floor." Neighbours were horrified by the damage. They stood along the police tape, shaking their heads and crying in grief. They could see into the home where the walls had burned away. Black, charred pieces of the house littered the lawn around a jungle gym in the backyard. The back of the house was blackened, with the blue siding melted off.

Kelly Grogan, 27, said she was lying in bed when she heard screams. "I remember it — the screeching," she said. "It really terrified me." "I looked out the window and the boy was standing on the roof yelling, `Help me. Help me.'" Jason Bevilaqua, 26, said his wife woke him up and told him there was a fire across the street and a boy was on the roof. He got his ladder out of the basement and ran to the burning home barefoot and in his pyjamas. "I couldn't hear anything that was being said," added Bevilaqua yesterday afternoon. "He was terrified, so I had to go up the ladder to get to him." Bevilaqua said he tried unsuccessfully to kick down the door. Thick, black smoke was billowing out the windows. Constable Kevin Giblin of the Montreal police said the neighbours' help was critical.

Firefighters arrived within minutes of the neighbours calling 911. Firefighter Sheldon Presting entered the home with a thermal imaging camera, which helped him see through the smoke. He found the sister in an upstairs bedroom and the two boys lying in their beds. CPR was performed on the two boys on the front lawn. They were taken to Hotel Dieu and Montreal General Hospital. The sister was airlifted to Ottawa Specialty Burn Unit.

Question 21

Because the children were lying in their beds, what is the most logical inference that can be made?

a) They were actively trying to save themselves.

b) They were overcome by smoke and probably unconscious when the fire made it to their room.

c) They started the fire on purpose.

d) Someone drugged them.

Question 22

Which children were in the house when the fire started?

a) Jarmin, Kaylin, Jaya and Dinesh   b) Jarmin, Kaylin, Kavi, and Jaya

c) Dinesh, Jarmin, Ali, and Jaya   d) Kavi, Jarmin, Dinesh, Jaya

Question 23

Which two children were most likely woken up by the fire?

a) Dinesh and Jarmin   b) Kaylin and Jarmin

c) Dinesh and Jaya   d) Jaya and Kaylin

Question 24

What heroic actions were taken to save Dinesh's life?

a) The front door was kicked in and he was brought out.

b) Someone caught him as he jumped off the second floor roof.

c) He was carried down a ladder from the second floor roof.

d) A firefighter with a thermal imaging camera rescued the boy.

Question 25

What hospital was not involved with this occurrence?

a) Montreal General Hospital   b) Montreal Specialty Burn Unit

c) Ottawa Specialty Burn Unit   d) Hotel Dieu

Answer questions 26 - 30 based on the following passage.

Dealing with short-tempered victims is one of the greatest challenges faced by emergency service personnel, such as paramedics, police and firefighters. Patience is one of the most important traits of emergency service personnel when they deal with complaints and abuse from victims. Remember that irate victims have been through tremendous stress and aren't necessarily angry with you. They may have lost all their worldly possessions, their health, or a close family member. They are projecting anger they feel about their situation onto you. The best course of action would be to remain calm, deal with them gently, and ignore any insults or hostilities they may have. Responding to them with hostility may only exasperate the situation, which can make it more difficult to gain information from them and provide adequate treatment to them. Their insults may be completely irrational, and the victims may not even be aware of what they are saying in their grief. They may even attempt to anger you in order to provoke a reaction from you. Attempt to remain calm and exercise patience in the matter. Otherwise, you may fail to get valuable information necessary to providing these victims with proper care.

Question 26

Exasperate in this paragraph means:

a) annoy, worsen

b) rectify, fix

c) amuse

d) sadden

Question 27

One general theme that the author is suggesting is:

a) Victims are always abusive.

b) Victims got what they deserved.

c) Victims are not in their normal state of mind.

d) Victims have the right to be abusive.

Question 28

What is one action that the author would probably not recommend from emergency personnel?

a) Accepting physical abuse from victims.

b) Remaining patient during a victim's rants.

c) Treating the victim professionally even if they get personal.

d) Accepting a few personal insults without responding.

Question 29

What would be the greatest concern with failing to deal with an upset victim properly?

a) Being sued for negligence.

b) Having an untreated victims health be put in jeopardy.

c) Getting in trouble with your supervisor.

d) Poor public perception.

Question 30

In the article, what is the reason given for victims being abusive toward emergency personnel?

a) They blame you for their loss.

b) They are unbalanced people.

c) They are attempting to get compensation through a lawsuit.

d) They are projecting their anger and grief onto you.

Answer questions 31 - 35 based on the following passage.

Conduction is the process in which thermal energy flows from one material to another through the direct contact of the two materials.

Convection is the process of heat transfer in a gas or liquid by the circulation of currents from one region to another. This process is used in convection ovens. A fire that begins at the base of a wall may create enough heat as it ascends that the ceiling eventually ignites based on the heat alone.

Radiation is the third form of thermal energy. Thermal energy, like light energy, travels in waves. This energy is absorbed by non-reflective material. If the heat the non-reflective material absorbs surpasses the material's ignition point, a fire can start.

As a rule, if two objects are placed together with different thermal energies, energy will flow from the hotter to the cooler material until equilibrium is achieved. Conduction, Convection and Radiation are the three processes by which heat is transferred between objects.

Question 31

A fire in one room is in direct contact with a heating duct. The increased heat of the duct causes a fire to start in a separate room. Which process started the second fire?

a) Convection and conduction   b) Radiation and conduction

c) Convection   d) Conduction

Question 32

What heat transfer process occurs when someone gets sunburned?

a) Conduction   b) Convection

c) Radiation   d) None of the above

Question 33

What would be an example of convection energy transfer?

a) Steaming vegetables on the stove.   b) Boiling rice on the stove.

c) Cooking popcorn in a microwave.   d) Heating water in a hot water tank.

Question 34

A fire breaks out at the bottom of a tower. Eventually, as the fire grows in size the ceiling becomes so hot it bursts into flames. What form of energy transfer does this represent?

a) Conduction   b) Convection

c) Radiation   d) Combination of radiation and convection

Question 35

According to the passage, which of the following statements is not true?

a) Expansion occurs as gasses and liquids are heated.

b) An equilibrium will eventually be reached between two materials with different temperatures.

c) A fire occurs if the thermal energy absorbed surpasses the material's ignition point.

d) Conduction is always the fastest energy transfer process.

Answer questions 36 - 40 based on the following passage.

The two main purposes of fire detection are reducing the risk to life and limb and reducing the risk of property damage. Timing is very important when fires break out in populated areas. Time is required not only to notify persons in the area of the imminent danger, but also to get people in that danger area to a safe location. That's one of the reasons that fire departments across North America recommend that every business and home have an escape plan in case a fire breaks out. Escape routes should also be made available and remain unobstructed.

Where the protection of property is the larger consideration, longer detection times are often tolerated to prevent needless alarms. Warehouses and storage facilities tolerate longer detection times than high-density residential units. Sprinkler systems are often used as both a detection device and a fire-fighting device.

Sprinkler systems, which are often heat activated, are not installed in homes. This means they will not respond to smouldering fires in a large building where smoke inhalation is a serious threat to peoples' lives. Home detectors are often the only tools used in residential houses. Recently, the law has also been requiring the installation of carbon monoxide detectors.

Question 36

What is a reason the article gives for sprinkler systems failing to respond to some fires?

a) Sprinklers are set to respond only when manually activated.

b) Some sprinkler systems respond only to temperature signals.

c) Sprinklers only detect carbon monoxide.

d) Sprinklers aren't built or tested very well.

Question 37

Time is extremely important to:

a) Protect personal belongings.

b) Relocate people at risk to safe areas.

c) Alert people involved of the danger.

d) Both B & C.

Question 38

According to the passage, fire detection is important for what reasons?

a) Protect property.   b) Notify help.

c) Protect lives.   d) All of the above.

Question 39

According to the passage, which statement is not true?

a) Carbon monoxide detectors are replacing fire alarms in homes.

b) Sprinklers are used to help fight the fire and detect the presence of fire.

c) Time is important to alert people and get them to a safe refuge.

d) Carbon monoxide detectors are becoming very important home tools.

Question 40

According to the passage, which of the following statements is not true?

a) Businesses and homes should have an escape plan in case of fire.

b) Escape routes should not be blocked.

c) You only require one escape route from each building.

d) Protection of property is not as important as protection of life.

Question 41

While performing a training exercise your supervisor orders you to climb an old ladder which you feel is unsafe and may break at any moment. What is the best course of action?

a) Do as you are told and ignore the danger.

b) Obey the order, but file a complaint at the end of your shift.

c) Point out the dangerous ladder to your supervisor and, for safety concerns, request a new ladder to be used.

d) Refuse to obey the order.

Question 42

Shortly after extinguishing a fire on the second floor of a private home, the owner complains to you about the damage to the front door and staircase. What action should you take?

a) Explain the reasons for the damage to the door and the staircase.

b) Tell the owner not to question your actions; you know what you are doing.

c) Tell the owner to fill out a complaint form.

d) Listen patiently, apologize and walk away.

Question 43

You've spoken to your captain about replacing some equipment in the firehouse. Several weeks later, the equipment hadn't been replaced. What is the best course of action?

a) Go to your captain's supervisor and complain.

b) File a grievance through the union.

c) Do nothing even though you feel you were treated unfairly.

d) Ask the captain if anything has been done about the equipment.

Question 44

You are a rookie on the job. While working with a senior firefighter he performs an action you do not understand or agree with. What is the best course of action?

a) Inform a supervisor about the senior officer's mistake.

b) After the situation is over, talk privately to the senior officer about the action taken, your concerns and lack of understanding.

c) Correct the senior firefighter in public.

d) Disregard the situation as it is not that important.

Question 45

You are at the scene of a serious fire that has just been extinguished. A newspaper reporter wants to ask you questions. What is the best course of action?

a) Tell the reporter everything you know about the fire.

b) Refer the reporter to your supervisor.

c) Improve public relations by emphasizing your hard work in the interview.

d) Order the reporter to leave and threaten to have him charged with trespassing.

Question 46

While on the scene of a serious fire you are ordered by your captain to carry a hose line up a fire escape to a second floor window. You feel that the fire escape is not entirely safe. What is the best course of action?

a) Disregard the order, as it is not a safe situation.

b) Request to have a second captain assess the situation.

c) Inform the captain you will only obey the order if you feel it is safe.

d) Obey the order.

Question 47

While fighting a fire your superior gives you an order which you fail to hear because of the noise and commotion of the situation. What should you do?

a) Ask her to repeat the order.

b) Ignore the order and continue with what you were doing.

c) Make your own decision concerning what you should do based on your training.

d) Ask another superior for an order.

Question 48

A new female firefighter, the first to work at your station, has just arrived to begin her duties. What is the most appropriate action to take?

a) Ignore her; she will make introductions when she wants to talk to you.

b) Be extra nice to her and offer to do her cleaning duties.

c) Introduce yourself and treat her as you would any other co-worker.

d) To help her fit in, play a prank on her when she arrives.

Question 49

You learn that one of your co-workers is undergoing severe financial hardships, which you feel may impact his work performance in the future. What is the best course of action?

a) Ignore the situation; it is his own fault for getting himself into difficulty.

b) Suggest that he speak to the financial planner you personally use.

c) Notify a supervisor of the situation.

d) Let the co-worker know you are available if he wishes to talk about the situation.

Question 50

You arrive on the scene of a violent domestic situation. A police officer orders you to stay out of the house, as it is not safe, and rushes into the house. What action should you take?

a) Rush in anyway because there is a woman within who may need medical assistance.

b) Tell the officer to come back and explain his order.

c) Obey the officer's order and wait till he informs you that the situation is safe.

d) Wait a minute and, if you feel things are safe, go in.

Question 51

While working at a community event you see a person with a disability having difficulty with their wheelchair. You should:

a) Approach the person and ask if they need assistance.

b) Walk up and push the chair to correct the problem.

c) Ignore the situation, someone else can deal with it.

d) Walk over and lift the individual out of the chair.

Question 52

At the end of a busy shift you are extremely tired and want to get home. A co-worker asks if you can cover for him for a couple of hours. You should:

a) Agree to work even though you are exhausted.

b) Yell at the co-worker for being so rude.

c) Tell your supervisor that your co-worker is being irresponsible.

d) Explain that you are too tired to continue working and need to get home.

Question 53

One of your coworkers has a tendency to play music too loud in the firehouse. It has never bothered you, but you realize it bothers some co-workers. What action should you take?

a) Tell the people who are bothered to report him to a supervisor.

b) Ignore the situation as you are not his supervisor and his actions do not bother you.

c) Take his stereo from him.

d) Inform the supervisor of the problem yourself.

Question 54

For several months personal property has been disappearing from the station house. One day you catch one of your co-workers going through someone else's locker. He doesn't see you but you observe him remove a watch from the locker and then close it. Later that day, Jim complains that his watch is missing. What should you do?

a) Do nothing; you do not want to be labelled a rat.

b) Confront your co-worker to let him know what you saw and encourage him to turn himself in.

c) Inform Jim what you saw.

d) Inform a supervisor immediately.

Question 55

While replacing a ladder after a training exercise you drop it and cause damage to one of the supports. You should:

a) Attempt to hide the damage, as the ladders are expensive.

b) Report the damage to a supervisor.

c) Ignore the damage, as someone else will see it and report it.

d) File a report that the ladder was damaged before you touched it.

Question 56

You are working as a firefighter and a man enters the station to report he has locked his keys in his vehicle. He asks for your help to get them out. You should:

a) Inform him to call a tow truck company and offer the use of the phone.

b) Grab some tools from the station and attempt to open the door.

c) Tell him not to waste the fire departments time.

d) Tell him you have a friend that can help for $20.

Question 57

While shopping off duty, you witness a woman beginning to have an apparent heart attack. Which action would be inappropriate?

a) Asking the staff of the store to dial 911 for assistance.

b) Beginning CPR despite lacking some equipment.

c) Leaving without providing assistance.

d) Calling 911 on your cell phone to get help there.

Question 58

While on the scene of a serious fire your captain orders you to check the rear of the building. It is important to know the location of the rear fire exits for the firefighters in the building. As you are doing this, the District Chief calls you over and orders you to remain with the trucks. What should you do?

a) Inform the Chief of your current order from your captain, as well as the reasons for it, and ask for direction.

b) Disregard the Chiefs' order, as your captain said the information about the rear of the building was important.

c) Obey the Chief, as he is a higher-ranking officer than your captain.

d) Go back to your captain and ask his opinion on the matter.

Question 59

You notice one of your co-workers regularly misusing the equipment used in fighting fires. What would be the best way to handle this situation?

a) Mention the misuse to you co-workers.

b) Advise him on the proper use of the equipment and inform a supervisor only if the problem persists.

c) Immediately report the misuse to a supervisor.

d) Ignore the situation, as you are not the co-worker's supervisor.

Question 60

Your supervisor orders you to watch the truck at a fire scene. While you are on your own a few minutes later, you see a structural support fall on a fellow firefighters' leg, pinning him. You are the only other person nearby. You should:

a) Call for assistance on the radio to help the fallen firefighter, but stay by the truck.

b) Follow the orders of your supervisor and protect the truck.

c) Call for assistance on the radio and assist the firefighter in trouble.

d) Order a civilian nearby to assist the firefighter.

Question 61

A firefighter must lift a box using a lever. Choosing from the diagram below, on which triangle should she place the pivot point to make the lift easier (reduce effort)?

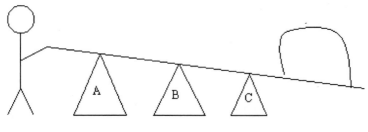

a) A

b) B

c) C

d) does not make a difference

Question 62

If a crow bar is used to lift a heavy box, as shown in the diagram below, how much effort is required to do the job?

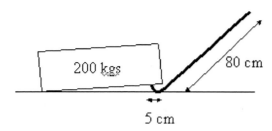

a) 10 kg

b) 5.5 kg

c) 15 kg

d) 12.5 kg

Question 63

In order to raise a 200 kg barrel to a 2-metre elevation you, will use a 10-metre ramp. How much effort is required to roll the barrel up the ramp?

a) 30 kg

b) 40 kg

c) 50 kg

d) 60 kg

Question 64

In the example below the box has to be lifted 2 metres. How much rope will have to be pulled through the pulley?

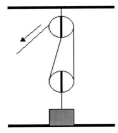

a) 1 metre

b) 2 metres

c) 3 metres

d) 4 metres

Question 65

Gear E in the diagram below begins to turn clockwise. This will cause gear B to turn:

a) Turn the same way as gear D

b) Turn clockwise

c) Turn the same way as gear C

d) Turn faster than gear E

Question 66

If gear A in the diagram below begins spinning clockwise, what will happen to the spring attached to the wall?

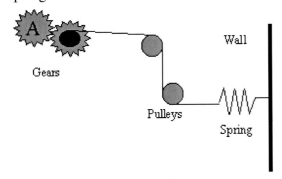

a) Nothing

b) The spring will be compressed

c) The spring will stretch

d) The spring will touch the gears

Question 67

What effect does crossing the belt have on the two pulleys, as outlined in the diagram below?

a) Speeds up pulley B

b) Slows down pulley B

c) Causes the two pulleys to spin in opposite directions

d) Causes the two pulleys to spin in the same direction

Question 68

In the diagram below, if wheel A spins at a rate of 4000 rpm, how fast will wheel D spin?

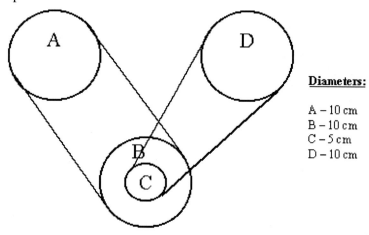

Diameters:

A – 10 cm
B – 10 cm
C – 5 cm
D – 10 cm

a) 4000 rpm

b) 8000 rpm

c) 2000 rpm

d) 1000 rpm

Question 69

What is the tool below best used for?

a) Cutting holes in panels

b) Cutting plastic

c) Cutting fine joints in wood

d) Cutting timber and felling trees

Question 70

Which of the following tools would be most useful to install bolts?

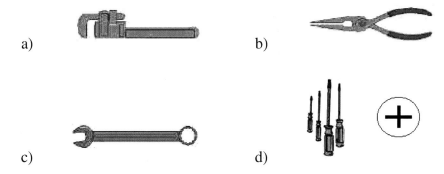

a)

b)

c)

d)

Question 71

Which of the following is not a measuring device?

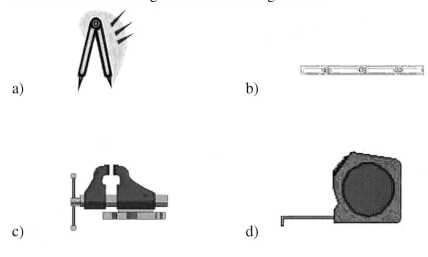

a)

b)

c)

d)

Question 72

Which of the following screws has a Phillip's head?

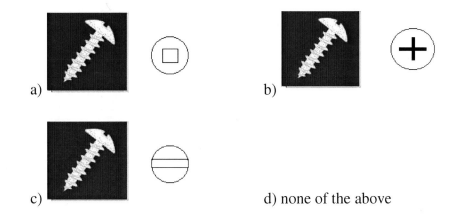

a)

b)

c)

d) none of the above

Question 73

Of the objects listed below, which one would most require the use of a crowbar?

a) Pipe   b) Brick wall

c) Battery   d) Crate

Questions 74 – 76 are based on the diagram below.

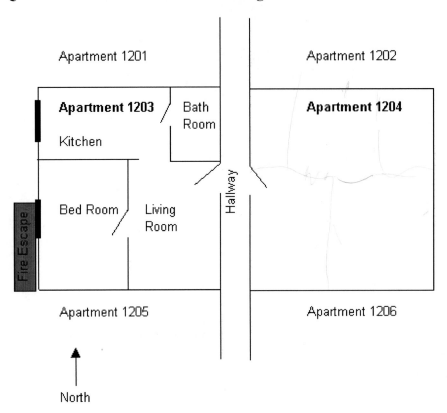

Apartments 1203 and 1204 are mirror images of each other. All of the apartments on the same side of the hall have the exact same floor plan.

Question 74

If firefighters have to enter apartment 1204 through the north window, where is the entrance to the living room located?

a) south/east corner of the kitchen   b) south/east corner of the bedroom

c) south/west corner of the kitchen   d) south/west corner of the bedroom

Question 75

All of the apartments on the west side of the hallway have the same layout as apartment 1203. If firefighters needed to drill a hole into the bedroom of apartment 1203 from apartment 1205, what room would they have to be in?

a) Bedroom   b) Kitchen

c) Bathroom   d) Living room

Question 76

A child is trapped in a fire in the northwest room of apartment 1202. Which room is this?

a) Kitchen

b) Bathroom

c) Bedroom

d) Living Room

Questions 77 – 80 are based on the map below.

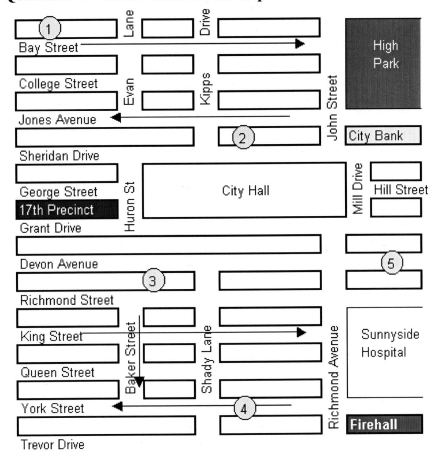

Question 77

What is the fastest legal route from Queen St. west of Baker St. to position 5?

a) Queen St. to Shady Lane, Shady Lane to Devon Ave., Devon Ave. to #5

b) Queen St. to Baker St., Baker St. to King St., King St. to Richmond Ave., Richmond Ave. to Devon Ave., Devon Ave. to #5

c) Queen St. to Richmond Ave., Richmond Ave. to Devon Ave., Devon Ave. to #5

d) Either A or C

Question 78

You receive a radio call about a fire in High Park. You receive the call while you are driving by the 17th Precinct. What is the quickest route there?

a) George to Huron, Huron to Sheridan, Sheridan to John, John to the location.

b) George to Huron, Huron to Grant, Grant to Mill, Mill to Sheridan, Sheridan to John, John to the location.

c) George to Huron, Huron to Sheridan, Sheridan to Kipps, Kipps to Jones, Jones to Evan, Evan to College, College to the location.

d) Either A or B

Question 79

While at position 1 you receive a radio call for a child hanging from a 4th floor window at position 2 on Jones Ave. Which route would you take?

a) Bay to John, John to Jones, Jones to the location.

b) Bay to Evan, Evan to College, College to John, John to Jones, Jones to the location.

c) Bay to Kipps, Kipps to Jones, Jones to the location.

d) Either A or B

Question 80

Which of the following locations is the easiest to get to from position 4?

a) Huron St. and George St.   b) Kipps Dr. and Bay St.

c) City Bank   d) Mill Dr. and Hill St.

Question 81

Kent put his loose change in a bottle. He put in 3 pennies, 6 quarters, 3 dimes and 1 nickel. What is the probability of picking out a quarter?

a) 23%   b) 8%

c) 33%   d) 46%

Question 82

A computer software package costs $27.91 at the local store. A customer gives 3 ten-dollar bills. How much change does the customer receive?

a) $1.89   b) $1.95

c) $2.09   d) $2.15

Question 83

Kevin determined that he could ski at the rate of 6 m in 1/5 of a second. How many meters could Kevin ski in 12 seconds?

a) 360 m   b) 380 m

c) 400 m   d) 420 m

Question 84

The perimeter of a room is 20 meters. Which of the following could be the area of the square?

a) 28 metres squared   b) 40 metres squared

c) 240 metres squared   d) none of these

Question 85

Which of the following represents fractions arranged in a decreasing order of size?

a) 0.003, 0.02, 0.1   b) 2/3, 1/4, 13/15, 3/5, 5/1

c) 15/16, 7/8, 3/4, 2/3, 1/2   d) none of these

Question 86

A crate full of wheat weighs 60 kg. If 4 1/3 kg of wheat is spilled out of the crate, how many kg does the remaining wheat weigh?

a) 55 1/3   b) 55 2/3

c) 56 2/3   d) none of these

Question 87

What is the volume of a cylinder with the following dimensions?

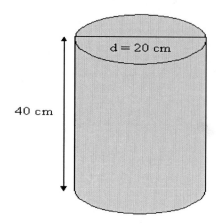

a) 12,560 cubed centimetres
b) 50,240 cubed centimetres
c) 75, 230 cubed centimetres
d) none of these

Question 88

Donovan can run 15 m in 2 seconds and Michael can run 20 m in 3 seconds. Who would win over 100 m and by how much?

a) Michael by 1.67 seconds
b) Michael by 2.32 seconds
c) Donovan by 1.67 seconds
d) Donovan by 2.32 seconds

Question 89

A phone cable 84 cm long is to be spliced to another piece one third as long. What is the length of the new cable?

a) 112 cm
b) 124 cm
c) 140 cm
d) 152 cm

Question 90

In the diagram below a ladder is leaning against a wall. What is the length of the ladder?

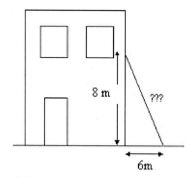

a) 8 m
b) 10 m
c) 12 m
d) Impossible to determine.

Question 91

A woman is 22 years older than her eldest son, and 29 years older than her youngest. If the youngest is now 7 years old, how old will the eldest be in 6 years?

a) 20   b) 19

c) 18   d) 17

Question 92

What is the volume of the figure below?

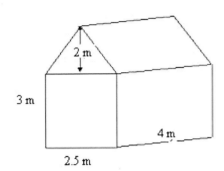

a) 30 cubed metres   b) 35 cubed metres

c) 40 cubed metres   d) 45 cubed metres

Question 93

There are 18 slices in a pizza. Mike ate ½ of the pizza. Jim ate 2/6 of the pizza. Daren ate the remaining slices. How many slices did Daren eat?

a) 5   b) 4

c) 3   d) 2

Question 94

Jane bought 4 DVD's at $6 each. She then found $9 on the street corner. She now has $59. How much money did Jane have before she bought the DVD's?

a) $74   b) $89

c) $90   d) $56

Question 95

Doug is responsible for filling out insurance requisitions at his office. In May, he was able to process 1,322 requisitions. In June, the number of requisitions completed fell by 15%. In July, he was able to improve on his June numbers by 17%. How many requisitions did Doug complete in July?

a) 1,300   b) 1,315

c) 1,348   d) 1,412

Question 96

Solve for "y". $15 + 3 - 2y = 7y + 3$

a) 1.67

b) 1.85

c) 2.14

d) 3.14

Question 97

Water flows through a damn at a rate of 550 litres in 12 seconds. How much will flow through in 3 seconds?

a) 137.5 litres

b) 142.6 litres

c) 153.8 litres

d) 170.4 litres

Question 98

Natasha works 5 hours a day, 35 hours a week. She earns $6 an hour. How much will she earn in 3 weeks?

a) $590

b) $606

c) $620

d) $630

Question 99

If you get 4 eggs per day, how many weeks will it take to get 364 eggs?

a) 13

b) 97

c) 18

d) 91

Question 100

Firefighter James is organizing equipment for the annual charity picnic. Below is a list of all of the prize equipment for which he is responsible.

Equipment	Quantity
Bicycles	20
Pairs of roller-skates	15
Barbie Dolls	100
Toy Cars	100

What formula would James use to calculate the total number of prizes available?

a) 20 + 15 + 100

b) 15 + 100(2) + 20

c) 20 + 15 + 100 + 100

d) Both B and C

Memory	
1)	C
2)	B
3)	A
4)	C
5)	D
6)	A
7)	D
8)	A
9)	D
10)	C
11)	B
12)	C
13)	D
14)	B
15)	D
16)	B
17)	A
18)	D
19)	C
20)	C

Reading Comp	
21)	B
22)	A
23)	C
24)	C
25)	B
26)	A
27)	C
28)	A
29)	B
30)	D
31)	D
32)	C
33)	A
34)	B
35)	D
36)	B
37)	D
38)	D
39)	A
40)	C

Work Relations	
41)	C
42)	A
43)	D
44)	B
45)	B
46)	D
47)	A
48)	C
49)	D
50)	C
51)	A
52)	D
53)	B
54)	D
55)	B
56)	A
57)	C
58)	A
59)	B
60)	C

Mechanical Apt.	
61)	C
62)	D
63)	B
64)	D
65)	A
66)	C
67)	C
68)	C
69)	A
70)	C
71)	C
72)	B
73)	D
74)	C
75)	B
76)	B
77)	D
78)	A
79)	C
80)	D

Mathematics	
81)	D
82)	C
83)	A
84)	D
85)	C
86)	B
87)	A
88)	C
89)	A
90)	B
91)	A
92)	C
93)	C
94)	A
95)	B
96)	A
97)	A
98)	D
99)	A
100)	D

DETAILED ANSWER SOLUTIONS

There are no detailed solutions for questions 1 – 40.

Question 41

C - Point out the danger posed by the ladder to your superior and, for safety concerns, request a new ladder to be used.

Options A and B will still put your life in danger during a non-emergency event. Option D fails to communicate to your supervisor the problem with the order you wish to resolve. Option C will communicate your concerns to your captain, who may be unaware of the condition of the ladder. This would be the best first course of action. If this fails then option B or C would be possible choices.

Question 42

A - Explain the reasons for the damage to the door and the staircase.

Communication skills are essential for a firefighter, especially while interacting with the public on an emergency scene. The victim in this matter is not upset with the individual firefighter; they are upset with the situation they have found themselves in. An explanation might calm them down and allow them to understand the nature of the situation.

Answer B would be inappropriate and might escalate the situation. Answer C might initiate a needless procedure at this stage. Answer D fails to educate a member of the public about the potential damage fire can inflict, and also accepts undo responsibility for the situation.

Question 43

D - Ask the captain if anything has been done about the equipment.

Answers A and B would be inappropriate because you do not have any information as to what your captain did with your request for new equipment. Answer C would fail to resolve the issue of replacing the necessary equipment. Answer D will provide you with information such as whether action was taken to get the new equipment, whether your captain forgot to take action, or whether your captain felt no action was warranted. After you have this information a better decision can be made.

Question 44

B - Privately talk to the senior officer about the action taken, your concerns and lack of understanding after the situation is over.

It would be improper to correct a senior firefighter or complain to a supervisor about a situation you do not fully understand. Senior firefighters have more skill and experience, and should be used as a source of information and teaching. Pulling the firefighter aside to clarify the situation will help you learn. Other options should be taken if, at this stage, you feel a gross error was made, but not before. Option D is incorrect as it fails to address the need to learn what should be done in these situations.

Question 45

B - Refer the reporter to your supervisor.

Remember to keep your priorities in order when answering these questions. Talking to the reporter while you are handling an emergency situation would be inappropriate (A and C). The scene takes precedence. As a firefighter you should never lose your temper in public and begin yelling at civilians. Simply tell the reporter to speak to a supervisor and resume your duties.

Question 46

D - Obey the order.

It is important to distinguish between emergency and non-emergency situations. Firefighters must obey orders during emergency situations, even if they can place your life in danger. Face it, being ordered into a burning building to fight a fire is never a safe situation. Answer C would be a gross error in judgment in any situation. Going to a second captain to assess the situation would violate the chain of command.

Question 47

A - Ask her to repeat the order.

During emergency situations you may be given orders and your captain will expect them to be carried out. The captain will be issuing orders to other people with the expectation that you did as you were told. To ignore the order could be dangerous (B and C). Approaching another supervisor would violate the chain of command and could lead to the same problems as choices B and C. Simply ask her to repeat the order and clarify any areas of confusion - A.

Question 48

C - Introduce yourself and treat her as you would any other co-worker.

Joining a new fire station is always a little intimidating. It would be especially difficult to be the first female firefighter to ever work at a station. Because you are in a comfortable environment, and she is in a new environment, choice A would not be the best solution. Choice B could make her feel awkward as she would be receiving special treatment. Choice D could make her feel very awkward. Being polite, friendly and treating her like everyone else is the best solution – C.

Question 49

D - Let the co-worker know you are available if he wishes to talk about the situation.

Choice A is not the most appropriate option. When you see a co-worker is having difficulty, ignoring the situation may just aggravate the problem. Choice B, although better than choice A, would be intrusive into your co-workers life. There is no need to speak to a supervisor in this situation, as there hasn't been any problem with his work performance. Letting your co-worker know that you are available should he need assistance is the best option.

Question 50

C - Obey the officer's order and wait until he informs you the situation is safe.

It is important to distinguish between emergency and non-emergency situations. Firefighters must obey orders during emergency situations. Although there may be a woman in trouble inside, the police have informed you that the area is not safe. Because proper personnel are handling the emergency at this time, A is not a valid option. B is also not an appropriate response because it is obvious that he is required inside and doesn't have time at present to explain the order to you. D is also inappropriate. You have no idea what is occurring inside the building, while the police do. You could end up walking into a hostage situation in which someone is armed with a gun. Wait until police advise you the scene is safe before proceeding.

Question 51

A - Approach the person and ask if they need assistance.

Options B and D are overly intrusive and fail to respect the wishes of the individual having problems. You could ignore the situation and leave it to someone else, but in this case asking them if they need a hand is both polite and respectful.

Question 52

D - Explain that you are too tired to continue working and need to get home.

Even though teamwork is vital to being a firefighter, there are times when you have to tend to yourself. Working while exhausted is dangerous not only to yourself, but to your co-workers as well. Option A would be inappropriate. Option B and C would also be inappropriate. You co-worker has no idea how you are feeling at the moment. There is no need to become upset, or talk to a supervisor.

Question 53

B - Ignore the situation as you are not his supervisor and his actions do not bother you.

There are bound to be problems such as this when firefighters work closely together. This situation doesn't affect you at all. Options A and D are inappropriate as the people affected can speak to a supervisor if they wish. Option C is inappropriate as you are not the supervisor in charge of the station.

Question 54

D - Inform a supervisor immediately.

Theft is a serious offence at a fire station and should never be tolerated. It is the responsibility of a supervisor to handle these situations. They should be made aware of theft immediately.

Question 55

B - Report the damage to a supervisor.

Options A and C could lead to other firefighters injuring themselves by using a damaged ladder. Option D is dishonest and completely inappropriate.

Question 56

A - Tell him to call a tow truck company and offer the use of the phone.

Option B would not be appropriate because it is not in the mandate of the fire department to open car doors. You lack the training involved and may cause damage to his car, for which you would be liable. Options C and D would be inappropriate as they would both damage the public's perception of the fire department. Option A provides the assistance the man needs.

Question 57

C - Leaving without providing assistance.

Be careful about the wording of these questions if you got this answer incorrect. The question asks for an **inappropriate** action. Choices A, B, and D all address the need to assist the person. Choice C is the only option because it completely neglects the woman's need for assistance.

Question 58

A - Inform the chief of both your current order from your captain, and the reasons for it, and ask for direction.

In an emergency situation, such as the one in this case, decisions have to be made quickly and there are often several decision makers. The chief is the commanding officer of the scene and his orders have to be obeyed. This being the case, the chief should know of the situation so he can make informed decisions. Let the chief know about your previous order, then decide what course of action is most appropriate.

Question 59

B - Advise your co-worker on the proper use of the equipment and inform a supervisor only if the problem persists.

Option A would only cause bad blood among co-workers. It isn't appropriate to spread rumours or discuss the inadequacies of co-workers behind their backs. Option C is possible, but not the best option in this case. Option D is inappropriate as it fails to address the problem at hand, and the misuse may continue. Your co-worker may not be aware of how to properly use the equipment. Option B will correct this problem.

Question 60

C - Call for assistance on the radio and assist the firefighter in trouble.

You have to remember that things can change very quickly on the scene of a fire. When you were given the order, there were no firefighters who needed immediate assistance. Option B and C would be inappropriate, as your co-workers life is in danger and he requires immediate help. Option D would be inappropriate, as civilians lack the training you do in this situation and may injure themselves in the process of helping. Calling for additional help, and then reacting yourself, is the most appropriate action.

Question 61

The closer the pivot point is to the weight that has to elevated, the easier it is to lift the weight. However, keep in mind that as you gain mechanical advantage by moving the pivot point closer to the object, you lose potential height on the lift.

Question 62

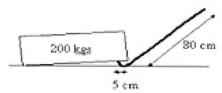

The formula for the mechanical advantage of a lever is:

Effort x (Distance 1) = Resistance x (Distance 2)

Effort x (80) = 200 x (5)
Effort x (80) = 1000
Effort = 1000 / 80   (divide both sides by 80 to isolate effort)
Effort = 12.5 kg

Question 63

The formula for the mechanical advantage of an inclined plane is:

Effort x (Length) = Resistance x (Height)

Effort x (10) = 200 x (2)
Effort x (10) = 400
Effort = 400 / 10   Divide both sides by 10 to isolate effort.
Effort = 40 kg

Question 64

The mechanical advantage in this pulley is 2:1 as the weight is evenly distributed across two ropes. This will reduce the weight by 50% but will also reduce the height of the lift by 50%. You will need twice as much rope to cover the same distance, or 4 metres of rope to lift the object 2 meters.

Question 65

Gears in direct contact will spin in opposite directions. If Gear E is turning clockwise, the following will occur:

Clockwise: Gear A, Gear C, and Gear E

Counter Clockwise: Gear D and Gear B

It is often easier to draw arrows on the gears to keep track of which way they are spinning.

Question 66

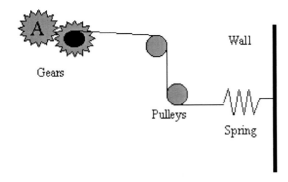

As Gear A turns clockwise, the gear it touches will turn counter clockwise, thereby pulling the rope. The ropes' direction of force is shifted by the pulleys in a manner that will pull the spring from the wall. As springs are pulled, they stretch.

Question 67

Since the wheels are the same size, their speeds will not be affected by crossing the ropes. Crossing them simply changes the direction of one of the wheels causing the two to spin in opposite directions.

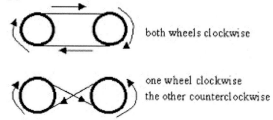

both wheels clockwise

one wheel clockwise
the other counterclockwise

Question 68

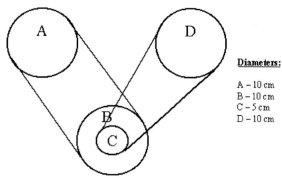

Diameters:

A – 10 cm
B – 10 cm
C – 5 cm
D – 10 cm

1) Wheel A will spin at the same speed as wheel B, as they are the same size and directly connected.
2) Wheel C will have the same RPM as wheel B (4,000 rpm).
3) Because wheel D is twice the size as wheel C it will only spin half a turn for each compete turn of wheel C. The turning rate is reduced by 50%.

$$4,000 / 2 = 2,000 \text{ rpm}$$

Question 74

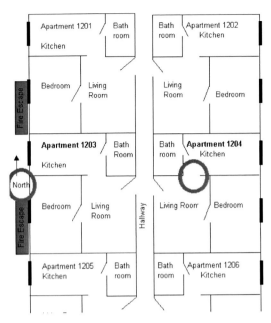

Question 75

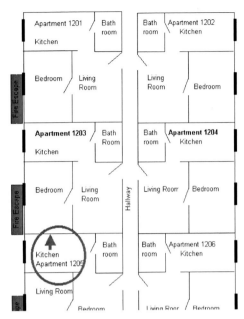

Question 76

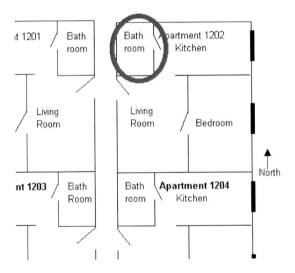

Question 77

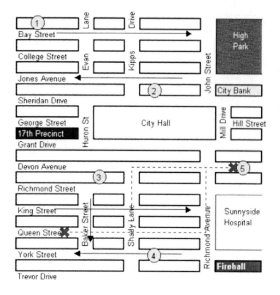

Question 78

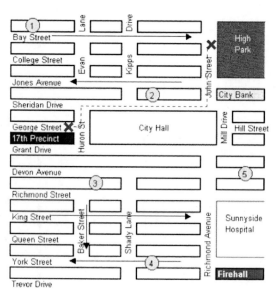

Question 79

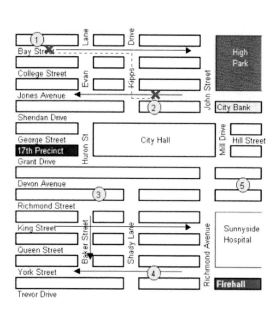

Question 80

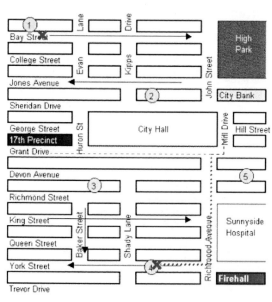

You basically have to drive by Hill Street and Mill Street to get to any of the other positions. It is the shortest distance.

Question 81
The total number of coins Kent put in the bottle was 13 (3 + 6 + 3 + 1). If there were 6 quarters then he has a 6 in 13 chance of picking out a quarter.

$$6 / 13 = 46\,\%$$

Question 82
The customer paid $30 (3 x 10) for the package. He should therefore receive $2.09 change.

$$\$30.00 - \$27.91 = \$2.09$$

Question 83
If Kevin can ski 6 m in 1/5 of a second, then he can ski 30 m per second (6 x 5). Therefore, in 12 seconds he could ski 360 m.

$$12 \times 30 = 360 \text{ m}$$

Question 84
If the room was a square and its perimeter is 20 meters, then each side would have to be 5 metres (20 / 4 = 5). Area is calculated by multiplying base x height (5 x 5 = 25 metres squared).

Question 85
15 / 16 =   45 / 48
7 / 8   =   42 / 48
3 / 4   =   36 / 48
2 / 3   =   32 / 48
1 / 2   =   24 / 48

Question 86
60 − 4 1/3 = 55 2/3 kg. The remaining wheat would weigh 55 2/3 kg.

Question 87

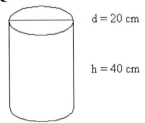

d = 20 cm

h = 40 cm

Volume of a cylinder = πr^2 x height

$\pi = 3.14$
r = 10 cm (radius is half the diameter)
h = 40 cm

$v = 3.14 \times 10^2 \times 40$
$= 3.14 \times 100 \times 40$
$= 314 \times 40$
$= 12{,}560 \text{ cm}^3$

Question 88

Donovan will run 100 metres in 13.33 seconds (100 x 2) / 15 = 13.33 seconds.
Michael will run 100 metres in 15 seconds (100 x 3) / 20 = 15 seconds.
Donovan will therefore win the race by 1.67 seconds (15 – 13.33 = 1.67).

Question 89

One third of 84 cm is 28 cm (84 / 3 = 28). The new cable will therefore be 112 cm (28 + 84 = 112 cm).

Question 90

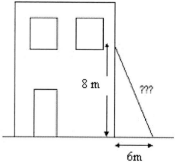

The Pythagorean theorem is required to solve this problem. The theorem states that in a right angle triangle the square of the side opposite the right angle equals the sum of the squares of the other two sides. The equation is:

$A^2 + B^2 = C$

C /| A
/_|
B

Fill the known values in the equation and solve for the unknown.

$8^2 + 6^2 = C^2$
$64 + 36 = C^2$
$100 = C^2$
C = 10 metres (the square route of 100 is 10 or 10 x 10 = 100)

Question 91

There is a 7-year difference in age between the woman's two sons (29 – 22 = 7). If the youngest son is now 7-years-old, the eldest would now be 14 (7 + 7 = 14). In six years the eldest will be 20 (14 + 6 = 20).

Question 92

What is the volume of the figure below?

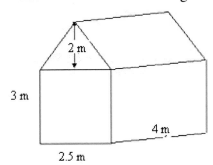

For this problem, break the object into two parts, calculate the volumes and add the results together. The first object is a cube.

Volume of a cube = length x width x height
= 4 x 2.5 x 3
= 10 x 3
= 30 m ^{3}

The volume of the top portion is determined by calculating the area of the triangle and multiplying it by the length of the object.

Area of a triangle = ½ x base x height
= 1/2 x 2.5 x 2
= 1/2 x 5
= 2.5 m ^{2}
Volume = 2.5 x 4 = 10 m ^{3}

Question 93

This question involves multiplication, division, addition and subtraction. The first step is to determine how many slices Mike and Jim ate.

18 total slices

1 / 2 - Mike

2 / 6 - Jim

To determine the number of slices each had, multiply the fraction by the total number. This is a two-stage process.

$18 \times \dfrac{1}{2} = \dfrac{18}{2}$ $18 \times \dfrac{2}{6} = \dfrac{36}{6}$

Multiply the numerator in both questions by 18. The denominator remains the same. After this, divide the numerator by the denominator.

$\dfrac{18}{2} = 9$ $\dfrac{36}{6} = 6$

Mike had 9 slices and Jim had 6 slices. Adding them together reveals that 15 slices have been eaten. This is now a subtraction problem.

18 total slices with 15 already eaten.
$$18 - 15 = 3 \textbf{ (C)}$$

Question 94

To solve this problem, work backwards using subtraction and multiplication.

$ 59 now
$ 9 found on corner
$24 spent on DVD's ($6 x 4 = $24)

Starting with the $59, subtract the $9 that Jane found because she did not have that before she bought the DVD's.

$$\$59 - \$9 = \$50$$

Then add back the money she spent on the DVD's. This will give you the answer.

$$\$50 + \$24 = \$74 \textbf{ (A)}$$

Question 95

Step 1: Determine the number of requests that were processed in June. This is accomplished by multiplying the number of requests in May by the percentage that the number dropped and then subtracting the two numbers from the May number.

```
  1 3 2 2          1 3 2 2
x   0. 1 5       -   1 9 8
    1 9 8          1 1 2 4 requests in June
```

Step 2: Determine the number of requests processed in July. This is accomplished by multiplying the number of requests in June by the percentage that the number increased. Then add the two numbers.

```
  1 1 2 4          1 1 2 4
x   0. 1 7       +   1 9 1
    1 9 1          1 3 1 5 requests in July (B)
```

Question 96

Step 1: Subtract 3 from both sides of the equation.

$$15 + 3 - 3 - 2y = 7y + 3 - 3 \qquad \text{or} \qquad 15 - 2y = 7y$$

Step 2: Add 2 y to both sides of the equation.

$$15 - 2y + 2y = 7y + 2y \qquad \text{or} \qquad 15 = 9y$$

Step 3: Isolate "y" by dividing both sides by 9.

$$\frac{15}{9} = \frac{9y}{9} \qquad \text{or } 1.67 = y \textbf{ (A)}$$

Question 97

This will require the use of fractions. Start by setting up an algebraic equation. In 12 seconds, 550 litres will flow. By assuming that the flow rate will not change, you can establish a relationship between the time and the water flow.

$$\frac{3}{12} = \frac{y}{550} \qquad \text{3 / 12 can be rewritten as 1/4 .}$$

This makes the calculations easier.

$$\frac{1}{4} = \frac{y}{550} \qquad \text{Isolate "y" by multiplying both sides of the equation by 550.}$$

$$\frac{550}{4} = y \qquad \text{550 / 4 = 137.5 litres } \textbf{(A)}$$

Question 98

Many word problems try to fool you with irrelevant information. Determine what information is necessary to solve the problem and discard the rest.

5 hours per day
35 hours per week
$6 an hour
3 weeks total

Here, the number of hours per day is not needed to solve the problem. It is a distraction.

This is a multi-step multiplication problem. Determine how much money is made in one week and then multiply by the number of weeks worked.

1) 35 x $6 = $210

2) $210 x 3 = $630 **(D)**

Question 99

This problem involves both multiplication and division skills. The first step is to determine how many eggs are received in a week. This is accomplished by multiplying the number of eggs per day by 7 days.

$4 \times 7 = 28$

Next, divide the number of eggs per week by the total number of eggs. The result is the solution to the problem.

```
              1 3 (A)
    2 8 ⌐ 3 6 4
         -2 8
             8 4
           - 8 4
               0
```

Question 100

This problem requires basic addition skills. To calculate the total number of prizes, add the numbers of each prize together.

$20 + 15 + 100 + 100 = 235$ **(D)**

It doesn't matter in which order the numbers appear. This equation could be restated any of the following ways:

$20 + 100 + 15 + 100 = 235$

$100 + 15 + 20 + 100 = 235$

There are also two like terms in this problem (100). It is possible to restate the formula in this manner:

$20 + 15 + 2(100) = 235$

Again, it doesn't matter in what order the numbers appear, so long as the like terms are multiplied together.

$15 + (100 \times 2) + 20$ ✓ $2 \times 100 + 15 + 20$ ✓

$2 \times 15 + 100 + 20$ ✗ $2(100 + 15 + 20)$ ✗

The CPS practice tests contain five sections. Start with Section 1 - Memory and work your way through the remaining sections (comprehension, work relations, mechanical reasoning and arithmetic reasoning).

The memory questions are based on the passage on page 144. Have a friend read the passage to you once from start to finish at a normal pace without repeating any portions. For the memory component, you are not permitted to take any notes.

The only material you can use is a pencil and scrap paper. No calculators, books, or counting devices. After the memory passage has been read, give yourself ninety minutes to complete the exam.

Memory

	A	B	C	D
1)	○	○	○	○
2)	○	○	○	○
3)	○	○	○	○
4)	○	○	○	○
5)	○	○	○	○
6)	○	○	○	○
7)	○	○	○	○
8)	○	○	○	○
9)	○	○	○	○
10)	○	○	○	○	___ / 20
11)	○	○	○	○
12)	○	○	○	○
13)	○	○	○	○
14)	○	○	○	○
15)	○	○	○	○
16)	○	○	○	○
17)	○	○	○	○
18)	○	○	○	○
19)	○	○	○	○
20)	○	○	○	○

Reading Comp

	A	B	C	D
21)	○	○	○	○
22)	○	○	○	○
23)	○	○	○	○
24)	○	○	○	○
25)	○	○	○	○
26)	○	○	○	○
27)	○	○	○	○
28)	○	○	○	○
29)	○	○	○	○
30)	○	○	○	○	___ / 20
31)	○	○	○	○
32)	○	○	○	○
33)	○	○	○	○
34)	○	○	○	○
35)	○	○	○	○
36)	○	○	○	○
37)	○	○	○	○
38)	○	○	○	○
39)	○	○	○	○
40)	○	○	○	○

Work Relations

	A	B	C	D
41)	○	○	○	○
42)	○	○	○	○
43)	○	○	○	○
44)	○	○	○	○
45)	○	○	○	○
46)	○	○	○	○
47)	○	○	○	○
48)	○	○	○	○
49)	○	○	○	○
50)	○	○	○	○	___ / 20
51)	○	○	○	○
52)	○	○	○	○
53)	○	○	○	○
54)	○	○	○	○
55)	○	○	○	○
56)	○	○	○	○
57)	○	○	○	○
58)	○	○	○	○
59)	○	○	○	○
60)	○	○	○	○

Mech. Aptitude

	A	B	C	D
61)	○	○	○	○
62)	○	○	○	○
63)	○	○	○	○
64)	○	○	○	○
65)	○	○	○	○
66)	○	○	○	○
67)	○	○	○	○
68)	○	○	○	○
69)	○	○	○	○
70)	○	○	○	○	___ / 20
71)	○	○	○	○
72)	○	○	○	○
73)	○	○	○	○
74)	○	○	○	○
75)	○	○	○	○
76)	○	○	○	○
77)	○	○	○	○
78)	○	○	○	○
79)	○	○	○	○
80)	○	○	○	○

Mathematics

	A	B	C	D
81)	○	○	○	○
82)	○	○	○	○
83)	○	○	○	○
84)	○	○	○	○
85)	○	○	○	○
86)	○	○	○	○
87)	○	○	○	○
88)	○	○	○	○
89)	○	○	○	○
90)	○	○	○	○	___ / 20
91)	○	○	○	○
92)	○	○	○	○
93)	○	○	○	○
94)	○	○	○	○
95)	○	○	○	○
96)	○	○	○	○
97)	○	○	○	○
98)	○	○	○	○
99)	○	○	○	○
100)	○	○	○	○

Sean Kavanaugh reported to Firehall #3 in Pickering Township for his day of work at 7:30 am. He drove to work from his home at 718 Glen Garden Gate, which is located in the City of Oshawa. He arrived at work at 7:15 am to relieve the night shift, which had a busy night with an industrial park fire.

Sean reported directly to his captain, James Jessop, who was in charge of Pumper #6. Other people who would be working on Sean's truck that day included Kavi, Nigel and Brandon. Brandon was the driver of the day. The fire hall had three pumpers, an aerial truck and a hazardous materials unit. The entire day shift had a briefing meeting at 8:00 am. Sean was detailed to cleaning duties and instructed to clean Pumper # 6.

At 10:30 am a call came for a medical collapse at 17 Richmond Street East. Pumper #6 was dispatched to it. Sean suited up with his co-workers and headed for the call. While enroute they were advised that a 79-year-old man was having difficulty breathing and had fallen at the back of a grocery store. Paramedics were also enroute. Pumper #6 arrived on the scene at 10:35 am, at the same time that Paramedic Unit #847 responded. There were several elderly people at the front of the store. Shannon Grogan was among them wearing a purple hat and coat. The firefighters and paramedics entered the store and found a Mr. Grant lying face down on the floor breathing slowly and shallowly. While the man was being worked on, his wife, Shelley Grant, informed Sean that her husband, Bill, is a diabetic and has not had anything to eat in several hours. The paramedics began to treat the patient and decided to transport him to Glenview Hospital. The fire department was no longer needed on the call.

As Pumper #6 advised dispatch that they were heading back to the hall they were notified of another call for a fire in progress and ordered to join Pumper #5 and Aerial #3 at 615 Adelaide Street East. The time of this call was at 11:10 am. There were reports of smoke coming from the 5th floor of a small apartment building at that location. The building was being evacuated and the other units were enroute. At 11:20 am Pumper #6 pulled up to the building. Pumper #5 and Aerial #3 were already on the scene. A group of children, whose names were Jamal, Keith, and Michael, were standing across the street.

The superintendent, Sheldon, advised Sean that all apartment units had been notified of the fire except unit #7 on the fifth floor, which hadn't respond to the superintendent's knocking at the time. Sean was advised that the residents of unit #7 were a single mother who normally works during the day and her three children, Shayna, Kaylene, and Kal.

Captain Jessop ordered Sean to get the line ready and enter the building with Brandon and Nigel to double-check unit #7 for the three children. As Sean, Brandon and Nigel entered the building, they encountered a group from Pumper #5 exiting it. They advised that they had checked floors 2 and 4 and had extinguished visible flames on floor 4. They had exited because they had to refill their air supply. They reported no signs of any individuals in the apartment.

Sean, Brandon and Nigel climbed the southeast stairwell to the fifth floor and opened the door to heavy smoke, activated sprinklers and intense heat. They walked down the hall and approached the door to unit #7. After they banged on the door, a child's voice stated they weren't allowed to open doors to strangers. Nigel forced the door open, and the three firefighters entered the apartment. The room was filled with smoke but there was no visible fire. The child said her name was Shayna. The other children were hiding beneath their beds but were found quickly because of their choking. Sean and Brandon immediately provided air for the two other children.

When the firefighters looked back into the hall they saw the path they had followed to reach the unit had erupted into an inferno. The three firefighters grabbed the children and rushed to the stairwell on the north side of the building. They descended to the ground floor and immediately notified Captain Jessop of the children they rescued from the building and the location and spread of the fire.

The fire was brought under control at approximately 2:30 pm. Other units that were on the scene as the fire was extinguished included the aerial tower, 3 pumpers, the aerial and the district chief.

MEMORY COMPONENT

Question 1

What city was Sean Kavanaugh working for?

a) Pickering Township

b) City of Oshawa

c) City of Scarborough

d) Township of Markham

Question 2

At what time does the day shift start?

a) 7:00 am

b) 7:15 am

c) 7:30 am

d) 7:45 am

Question 3

Who is Sean's immediate supervisor?

a) Sergeant John Jessop

b) Captain Nigel Jessop

c) Captain John Jessop

d) Captain James Jessop

Question 4

Who was assigned to the same truck as Sean?

a) Kavi, Nigel, and Jamal

b) Kavi, Nigel, Brandon

c) Nigel, Brandon, Jamal

d) Nigel, Brandon, Jamal

Question 5

What is the location of the medical complaint?

a) 1543 Richmond Street

b) 17 Richmond Street

c) 615 Adelaide Street

d) 718 Glengarden Gate

Question 6

What information did the firefighters have when they were dispatched and enroute to the medical call?

a) Diabetic male with difficulty breathing

b) Medical collapse at 97 Richmond Street East

c) Elderly male suffering a heart attack

d) 79-year-old male with difficulty breathing

Question 7

What ultimately happened to Mr Grant?

a) Treated by paramedics and transported to Glenview Hospital

b) Treated by paramedics and released

c) Treated by paramedics and transferred to Mount Sinai Hospital

d) Treated by police and transported to Mount Sinai Hospital

Question 8
What floor was the smoke reported coming from enroute to the call?

a) 5th floor

b) 4th floor

c) 3rd floor

d) 2nd floor

Question 9
What street was the fire located on?

a) Richmond Street East

b) Richmond Street West

c) Adelaide Street West

d) Adelaide Street East

Question 10
What unit didn't the superintendent properly clear?

a) Unit 5 on the 7th floor

b) Unit 7 on the 5th floor

c) Unit 5 on the 5th floor

d) Unit 7 on the 7th floor

Question 11
How many children were reported as possibly still being in the apartment unit?

a) 1

b) 2

c) 3

d) 4

Question 12
Which of the names below was a child who could still be in the building?

a) Kal

b) Jamal

c) Keith

d) Karla

Question 13
What were Captain Jessop's orders?

a) Get a line ready and begin fighting the fire on the 5th floor.

b) Get a line ready and inspect the building starting on the 5th floor.

c) Get a line ready and double check for the three children.

d) Check for the three children right away.

Question 14
Who accompanied Sean into the building?

a) Brandon and Kavi

b) Brandon and Jessop

c) Kavi and Jessop

d) Brandon and Nigel

Question 15
What floors did pumper #5 check out?

a) Floors 2 and 4

b) Floors 1, 2 and 3

c) Floors 2 and 3

d) Floors 1 to 4

Question 16

Where did they extinguish visible flames?

a) Floor 2

b) Floor 3

c) Floor 4

d) Floor 5

Question 17

Which stairwell did they ascend?

a) Southwest stairwell

b) Southeast stairwell

c) Northwest stairwell

d) Northeast stairwell

Question 18

What did they encounter on the 5th floor?

a) No signs of fire.

b) Intense heat, active sprinklers and heavy smoke.

c) Intense heat, visible flames and several frightened animals.

d) None of the above.

Question 19

What alerted the firefighters to the children under their beds?

a) Choking

b) Crying

c) Exposed feet

d) Yelling

Question 20

What area of the building became on fire and prevented the firefighters from returning the way they came?

a) The front door of the apartment was on fire.

b) The southeast stairwell was on fire.

c) The hall was on fire to the south of them.

d) The living room of the apartment was on fire.

READING COMPREHENSION

Answer Questions 21 - 27 based on the following passage.

Gas leaks are extremely dangerous situations, especially in large urban areas. There populations are densely concentrated and any explosion could cause massive damage and a large number of personal injuries. Firefighters are trained to evacuate any area affected when a suspected flammable gas leak occurs. This would include evacuating a building of occupants.

If the location of a gas leak is determined, firefighters will open all possible doors and windows in order to create greater ventilation. One of the main priorities in these situations is to eliminate the threat. Once the location of the leak is determined the main valve should be shut off outside the building or, if that isn't possible, a valve inside the building feeding the leaking pipe should be closed. By checking the flow of the meter, firefighters will be able to determine if the leak has been terminated. If there is no gas flow registering than it is safe to assume the leak has stopped.

Sources of ignition must be contained. If there is a major gas leak in public, firefighters will order motorists turn their vehicles off and not start them again. The ignition process of starting a car causes some sparking which could ignite the gas in the area due to a leak. Preventing smoking is another obvious precaution that should be made by emergency personnel. Inside buildings lights should neither be turned on, nor turned off if they are already on. The act of flipping a light switch can cause a small electrical spark, which is all that is required to detonate the gas.

Once ignited, a fire is very difficult to put out until the source of the gas has been cut off. One major concern that firefighters may encounter is boiling liquid expanding vapour explosions (BLEVE). A BLEVE can occur if there is a gas tanker or a cylinder on fire due to a faulty relief valve, or even if there is a fire in the vicinity which is heating the contents of the tank. The heat causes the gas inside to expand rapidly. This increases pressure, which eventually has to be released through a massive explosion. Firefighters will aim a water stream at the tank not to extinguish the fire escaping from it but to cool the tank to prevent the gas from expanding and, thereby, eliminate the threat of a BLEVE.

Fire departments around the world have procedures in place to handle the dangerous situation of gas-related fires. Not all gases are easily detectable. Some are odourless and colourless, which require special instruments to detect.

Question 21

What is a method outlined to determine whether a gas flow has been stopped?

a) Checking the external valve for flow.

b) Checking the external meter for flow.

c) Opening windows to improve ventilation.

d) Shutting off all motor vehicle engines.

Question 22

According to the article above, what is not recommended?

a) Shutting off all lights in a suspected gas leak.

b) Cooling a gas cylinder with water if it is on fire or near a heat source.

c) Turning off motor vehicles in a gas leak area.

d) Evacuating a building where a gas leak has been confirmed.

Question 23

A firefighter sees fire escaping from gas pipe in a basement of a warehouse. The room has a large propane tank located near the fire. What strategy should be used in this case?

a) Water should be aimed at the tank to reduce the temperature of the gas inside.

b) An attempt should be made to shut off the valve feeding the pipe.

c) Both A and B.

d) Neither A nor B.

Question 24

Which of the following type of gas leak would pose the greatest risk?

a) Colourless and odourless gas leak

b) Gases with a strong pungent odour.

c) Gases that aren't flammable or toxic, such as helium.

d) Gases that are heavier than air.

Question 25

What steps should be taken when a firefighter encounters a gas leak?

a) Have all motor vehicles in an affected area turn off their engines.

b) Turn off all the lights in the area.

c) Evacuate the people in the area and then attempt to ventilate the affected area.

d) Both A and C.

Question 26

Which of the following is true of gas fires?

a) They are more dangerous than any other fire.

b) They only occur in buildings with natural gas piping.

c) They give off much more heat than any other type of fire.

d) None of the above.

Question 27

What do you feel is the first step when a gas leak is encountered?

a) Ventilate the area.   b) Evacuate all people.

c) Shut off all valves.   d) Notify the gas company.

Answer Questions 28 - 35 based on the following passage.

All too often we read tragic news stories of how people have died in house fires. When the house is inspected after the fire, the structure is often intact. Because the structure is basically intact, the question becomes: why were the occupants unable to escape to safety?

House fires are explained in detail in a recent article in the magazine *Fire Journal*. The article indicates that house fires react very differently than fires that occur outdoors, such as at fire pits at cottages. Burning branches for marshmallow roasts or logs in a fireplace is different than what occurs in a house fire. As the material is engulfed in flame, the heat escapes into the atmosphere. The fire spreads very gradually in what is termed a "friendly fire".

House fires are different because they are extremely "unfriendly". The key difference is that instead of the heat being lost to the atmosphere, the hot gases released are trapped inside the room. Within about one minute of a fire starting a layer of hot gases becomes trapped under the ceiling. The temperature in the room raises very quickly as the layer of gasses become thicker. Like a space heater, it begins to radiate its heat back down into the room. Everything in the room gets heated up extremely quickly. It is much easier for fire to spread to something that is already hot than something which is cold. Soon everything in the room is so hot that the fire "flashes over" from the original source of the fire, and everything in the room is set ablaze at once. This process can occur within as little as three minutes from the start of the fire. To repeat, room fires are more dangerous because the hot gases are trapped inside the room, unlike a fire outdoors. By the time flashover occurs, anyone in the room will be dead.

The effect of trapping the heat of a fire showed itself dramatically in a fire at a football stadium in Melbourne, Australia in 1973. Seventy-five people died when the whole structure erupted in flames. Later investigation showed that one of the reasons the fire spread so rapidly was that the roof of the stadium trapped the heat and smoke, just like the ceiling does in a house fire. Heat radiated back into the stadium led quickly to flashover.

News stories often describe people who are overcome when they attempt to fight a fire, or who go back into a burning home to retrieve possessions. This happens all of the time. Again, this is because of lack of awareness of how rapidly the heat builds up. By the time you have set up a garden hose outside, the fire is out of control.

Other problems in a house fire is the poisonous nature of several of the combustion products of domestic furnishings. Carbon monoxide, a colourless, odourless, but very poisonous gas, is formed whenever incomplete combustion takes place. It is especially hazardous because it makes you drowsy. When affected by it you are less likely to sense danger or take quick action. And, if you are asleep, you are less likely to waken. Synthetic materials such as foam cushions can release extremely toxic gases when they burn. These gases can include the poisonous material, hydrogen cyanide. These toxic gases quickly spread through the house, putting the other occupants at risk before they are in danger from the fire itself. An ongoing area of research is to manufacture furniture products that are comfortable, durable and safer in case of fire.

From what we have just read, we see that the problem of house fires in Canada has nothing to do with our use of wood as a construction material. The rapid spread of fire, the problem of flashback, and the danger to the occupants all take place long before the actual structure of the home is destroyed. The fire department may well be able to save the structure. Tragically, they may be too late to save the occupants. Smoke detectors remain our best method of sensing a fire soon enough to allow time to escape.

Question 28
What would be a good title to this article?

a) The Need for Steel Framed Houses.

b) Fire Department Response Times are Critical

c) Hazards of House Fires and the Need for Smoke Detectors.

d) The Call for Fire Friendly Furniture.

Question 29
As outlined in the article, what is the most significant difference between indoor and outdoor fires?

a) Heat retention.   b) Harmful gases.

c) Lack of control.   d) Open flames.

Question 30
What is a "flash over" as defined by this article?

a) Heat in the room causes material to spontaneously combust.

b) The tragic Melbourne fire of 1973.

c) The room temperature becomes so hot that material is ignited all at once from the original fire source.

d) Fire caused by a room full of gas, which erupts all at once.

Question 31
What are some of the hazards people face in house fires?

a) Poisonous gases.   b) Extreme heat.

c) Lack of awareness to the danger.   d) All of the above.

Question 32
What was one of the reasons for the quick spread of the fire in the Melbourne stadium in 1973?

a) Trapped explosive gas under the roof of the stadium.

b) Extremely combustible material.

c) Trapped heat and smoke under the roof of the stadium.

d) Both A and C.

Question 33

Which of the following structures would be at the greatest risk for a "flash over"?

a) Open roofed baseball stadium.   b) Yacht out to sea.

c) Children's playground.   d) Bush fire on a farm.

Question 34

What is not one of the effects of Carbon Monoxide inhalation?

a) It causes you to gag due to its strong odour.

b) It makes you drowsy.

c) It may prevent consciousness if you are sleeping.

d) Lessens your sense of danger.

Question 35

What does the author suggest is the most important means of protecting humans in the event of house fires?

a) Fire extinguishers.

b) More rapid response times from fire departments.

c) Carbon Monoxide detectors.

d) Smoke detectors.

Answer Questions 36 - 40 based on the following passage.

It is important for firefighters to recognize the different types of burns people can get. If they are unable to distinguish between the burns, they will not be able to effectively treat victims as each type of burn requires different treatments. It is very easy to remember the names of the burns. They are in order from least severe to most severe: first-degree, second-degree and third-degree burns.

First-degree burns cause the skin of the victim to turn red. Most mild sunburns are examples of first-degree burns. There is no blistering in first-degree burns and the only treatment that is required is to cool the burned skin with ice or cold tap water. This is the least serious of all burns.

Second-degree burns require immediate attention as they actually cause the blistering of the skin. The treatment involves immersing the burned area in warm water and then wrapping the affected area in a sterile dressing or bandage. You should not apply any butter or grease to these burns, as that may increase the chance of infections. If second-degree burns are limited to a small area of the victim they can be treated at home. If they cover a large area of the body the victim should be taken to a hospital immediately.

Third-degree burns occur when the skin is actually charred black or the skin turns white. These burns are most often caused by direct contact with flames or extreme heat. Chance of infection is very high with third-degree burns. Hospitalization is required immediately and water should not be applied. Any clothing that is attached should not be removed from the victim. If it is possible, any burn victim should be bandaged with a sterile dressing before being transported to the hospital.

Question 36

Which type of burn should be treated with ointments and lotions?

a) First-degree burns
b) Second-degree burns
c) Third-degree burns
d) None of the above

Question 37

Third degree burns turn the skin what colour?

a) Red or black
b) Black or white
c) Black
d) Red, white or black

Question 38

What burns may require hospitalization?

a) First degree burns
b) Second degree burns
c) Third degree burns
d) Second and third degree burns

Question 39

First-degree burns should be treated with:

a) cold water
b) warm water
c) ointment
d) sunscreen

Question 40

While a mother is boiling water on the stove her 5-year-old daughter spills the pot on herself. The skin on her face and both arms begins blistering almost immediately. What action is most appropriate?

a) Take the daughter to the hospital immediately.

b) Apply a sterile bandage to the burned area and head to the hospital.

c) Soak the burned area in warm water, apply a sterile bandage and head to the hospital.

d) Soak the burned area in warm water, then apply a sterile bandage.

Question 41

One afternoon several co-workers are relaxing upstairs when James tells a racist joke. At this time Dave leaves the room visibly upset. What is the most appropriate course of action?

a) Let it go. Dave will handle the situation himself.

b) Tell James not to make jokes like that in front of Dave.

c) Let James know that jokes like that are inappropriate and inform a supervisor.

d) Find Dave and tell him to lighten up.

Question 42

After extinguishing a major residential fire you are clearing some of the debris and putting it in a trash pile. The owner of the house comes over to you obviously upset and starts screaming at you for putting a burnt chair in a garbage pile. What should you do?

a) Apologize to the owner and ask him where you should place the chair.

b) Tell the owner that the chair is useless and to let you do your work.

c) Cease your efforts to clean up the area and tell the owner that he can handle the job if he wants to.

d) Ignore the owner and continue with your duties.

Question 43

While returning home from work you come across an accident in which a pedestrian was just struck by a car. The victim doesn't appear to be breathing and requires CPR. You recognize the victim as a local drug user. You do not have any emergency equipment with you. Which of the following statements is an inappropriate response?

a) Immediately call 911 to get emergency services dispatched.

b) Refuse to give CPR because you lack the equipment and you fear at risk of receiving a communicable disease.

c) Perform the duties you are capable of without putting yourself at risk to a communicable disease.

d) Perform CPR without proper equipment despite the fact that you feel you are putting yourself at risk of a communicable disease. This man needs help.

Question 44

While working at the station house you notice that Kevin has been coming in late for work several days in a row. This forces the people he is relieving to work late to ensure there is enough emergency personnel at the station. What statement is the most appropriate course of action?

a) Complain to your captain about the lack of respect Kevin has for his fellow coworkers.

b) Do nothing. This situation doesn't directly affect you and should be handled by those personally involved.

c) Take Kevin aside and tell him to show up to work on time.

d) Complain to other firefighters about Kevin's behaviour.

Question 45

You have been working for several months at a new station and Peter, one of your co-workers, continually teases you about your clothing style. At first you didn't mind, but now you are fed up with the constant belittling, especially in front of your other co-workers. What should you do?

a) Next time Peter makes a comment in front of your co-workers, publicly warn him to back off.

b) Pull Peter privately aside and ask him to lay off with the jokes.

c) Do nothing. You should get used to some teasing while working in this type of environment.

d) Talk to Peter and your captain about the situation.

Question 46

While at a serious fire, you yell out to Charles, one of your co-workers, asking for assistance with a ladder you are having trouble getting into position. Charles yells back that you aren't his boss and heads off without assisting you. You manage to get the ladder into place on your own and with a great deal of difficulty just in time to get a victim out of the building. What is an appropriate response?

a) Ignore this episode.

b) Inform your supervisor about the situation. Behaviour like this is inexcusable in emergency situations and has to be reported.

c) Complain to your fellow co-workers without mentioning it to your supervisor.

d) Talk to Charles later on and ask what the problem was.

Question 47

While responding to a fire call you determine that a pot left on the stove too long caused the smoke in the apartment. There is no fire, but there is dense smoke throughout the apartment. Your senior co-workers refuse to put on their protective air supply. What should you do?

a) Place your mask on and use the air supply to prevent breathing dangerous fumes while completing your work.

b) Order your co-workers to use their air supply as there is a significant health risk.

c) Follow your co-workers' example and perform your duties without protection.

d) Leave the apartment.

Question 48

Which of the following is the most serious offence a firefighter could commit?

a) Disregarding a direct order from a commanding officer.

b) Disorderly behaviour at the fire station.

c) Being under the influence of any illegal drug while on duty.

d) Failing to follow procedures in the line of duty.

Question 49

After extinguishing a fire you notice one of your co-workers involved in a heated exchange with a member of the public. You have no idea who started the verbal altercation or what it is about. The best course of action is to:

a) Approach the two parties to attempt to separate them and diffuse the situation.

b) Approach the situation and side with your co-worker. Have the member of the public removed from the area.

c) Ignore the situation; your co-worker can handle the situation.

d) Approach the situation and discipline your co-worker for arguing with a member of the public.

Question 50

You have been working as a firefighter for a number of years and your sister Jaya expresses interest in applying to the fire department for which you work. What actions would be inappropriate?

a) Encourage her to apply knowing she would be an excellent candidate.

b) Do not give her any support, as it would display favouritism.

c) Attempt to get her an official copy of the application test to help her study.

d) Both B and C.

Question 51

While responding to a fire call Sean, the driver, fails to stop for a red light and gets into an accident. When the police respond to investigate the accident Sean states that the light was green when he entered the intersection. What action should you take?

a) Pretend you didn't see what colour the light was.

b) Follow Sean's lead and inform the police officer that the light was green.

c) Pull Sean aside to tell him how you saw it, and let him know you will have to inform the officer of what you saw.

d) Refuse to give a statement to the officer.

Question 52

While searching a house for victims a fire spreads and blocks your exit. You are on the third floor and there is no fire escape. What should you do?

a) Call other firefighters for assistance.

b) Attempt to climb down the side of the building to avoid putting other firefighters at risk.

c) Attempt to fight the fire yourself to demonstrate your skills.

d) Wait for the fire to die down and then attempt the same exit.

Question 53

While evacuating victims from a burning building you come across an hysterical elderly male who is trying to save his favourite chair. The man is small in frame and appears to have difficulty walking. You should:

a) Respect the man's wishes to be left alone to get his chair out.

b) Pick up the man and immediately get him to safety.

c) Grab the man and have fellow firefighters bring his chair outside.

d) Move on to another part of the building to search for other victims who are more cooperative.

Question 54

You and two other firefighters are about to enter a burning warehouse from a fire escape when one of your co-workers slips and twists an ankle. What action would be inappropriate?

a) Get the firefighter to safety, and abort your plans to enter the warehouse at this time.

b) Call for assistance from other firefighters on scene to tend to your co-worker before entering the warehouse.

c) Order the firefighter to continue into the building with the original team.

d) Both A and C.

Question 55

While performing a safety inspection at a local apartment building you come across several serious infractions that warrant fines. The landlord asks you if there is anything he could provide you that would cause you to turn a blind eye to the infractions. What action is appropriate?

a) Issue the fines as required.

b) Caution the male against bribing a public official.

c) Inform your captain about the attempted bribe.

d) All of the above.

Question 56

You arrive at work and are feeling very ill with flu-like symptoms. The cold medication you have taken leaves you feeling drowsy and you are having a difficult time staying awake and alert. The shift is short firefighters this evening. What is the most appropriate action to take?

a) Inform your captain that you are too ill to continue your duties and book off sick.

b) Continue to work because the shift is short workers.

c) Inform your co-workers that you will work, but let them know you aren't feeling well.

d) Continue to work, unless a major incident occurs, then inform your captain you will be unable to handle the situation.

Question 57

After extinguishing a small fire in an abandoned first floor apartment you come across a case of expensive watches. You suspect that they are stolen. What should you do?

a) Notify the police without informing anyone else, as it might interfere with their investigation.

b) Keep the watches as they are abandoned material and belong to no one.

c) Notify your captain of the situation and your suspicion.

d) Split the watches among your coworkers.

Question 58

You are volunteering for a children's charity put on by the fire department. One of the organizers asks you to help her with something that only you can perform that will take about half an hour to complete. If you stay you will be late for work. What action should you take?

a) Call your captain and ask permission to arrive 20 minutes late for your shift.

b) Agree to do the work, as you are sure your captain won't mind if you are late for a good cause.

c) Inform the organizer that you have to leave in order to arrive at work on time.

d) Either A or C would be acceptable.

Question 59

Towards the end of your shift you see Dan acting suspiciously around Grant's equipment. You suspect that he is sabotaging the equipment. What course of action is most appropriate?

a) Confront Dan and warn him that if he does it again you will report him.

b) Report the incident to your captain.

c) Tell Grant to double check his equipment.

d) Do nothing. You only have suspicion at this stage and shouldn't act.

Question 60

While fighting a fire at a train station you come across a room packed with large gasoline cans. Fire has already broken out in the room and the gas cans are under intense heat. You should:

a) Leave the building immediately.

b) Immediately inform your supervisor and other firefighters.

c) Attempt to remove the cans from the dangerous area.

d) Continue fighting the fire as this is not an unusual situation.

Question 61

If a jackscrew handle is 30 cm long and the screw pitch is 1/3 of a cm, how much weight can be lifted by the jack with 10 kg of effort on the handle?

a) 5,652 kg

b) 6,562 kg

c) 3,540 kg

d) 4,860 kg

Question 62

A firefighter has to elevate a box (B) and uses a lever to do so. In order to make the lift easier, the firefighter should:

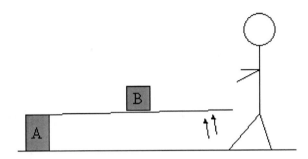

a) Move box B closer to herself.

b) Leave box B where it is.

c) Move box B closer to box A.

d) Moving box B will not have an impact on the effort required to lift it.

Question 63

In the diagram below two wheels attached by a belt drive have a 3:1 ratio. The smaller wheel has a 10 cm circumference. How fast would the smaller wheel turn if the larger one turned at a rate of 600 rpm?

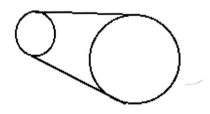

a) 1800 rpm

b) 600 rpm

c) 200 rpm

d) none of the above

Question 64

Of the three gears below, which one has the fastest rpm?

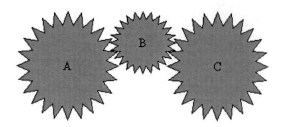

a) A

b) B

c) C

d) They all have the same rpm

Question 65

Which hose layout will produce the most efficient transport of water?

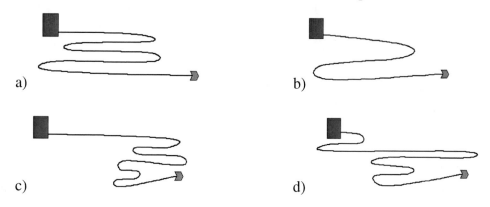

a)

b)

c)

d)

Question 66

Based on the picture below, which of the following statements is true?

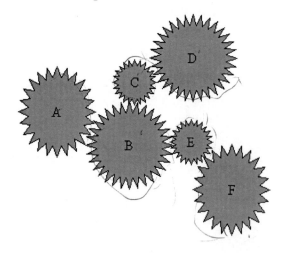

a) Gears A, C and F will all turn in the same direction.

b) If gear A turns clockwise, then so will gears C, E, and F.

c) If gear E turns clockwise, then gear C will turn counter clockwise.

d) Gears D and B will turn clockwise if gear F is turning clockwise.

Question 67

Which of the following tools is most appropriate for cutting sheet metal?

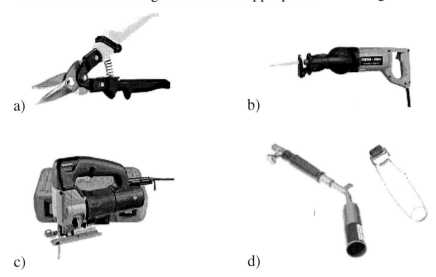

a)   b)

c)   d)

Question 68

What would be the most suitable use for the tool below?

a) Punching a hole through drywall.

b) Picking a lock.

c) Cutting a section of glass from a window.

d) Fastening a bolt.

Question 69

Which of the following tools is not a form of pliers?

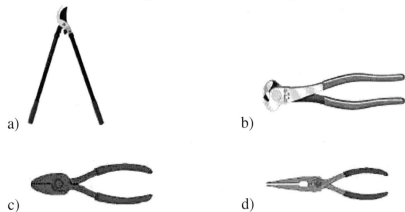

a)   b)

c)   d)

Question 70

Which type of saw would best be used to cut through plastic piping?

a) Hand Saw

b) Coping Saw

c) Chain Saw

d) Back Saw

Question 71

What is the primary use of this power tool?

a) Smooth a wooden surface

b) Sharpen other tools

c) Cut various grooves and moldings

d) Fasten joints together

Question 72

Which of the following tools would most likely be used with this:

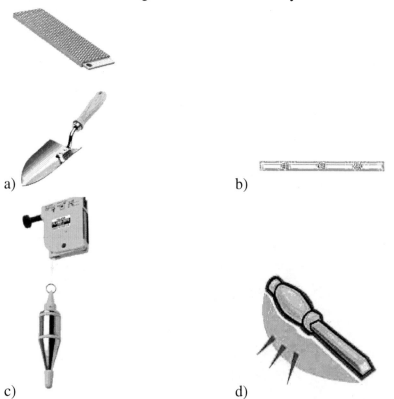

Question 73

Which tool would you select for precise measurements less than 100 mm or 6 inches?

a) Inside Calipers

b) Outside Calipers

c) Micrometre Calipers

d) Vernier Calipers

Question 74

Which of the following tools would be most useful for removing a padlock?

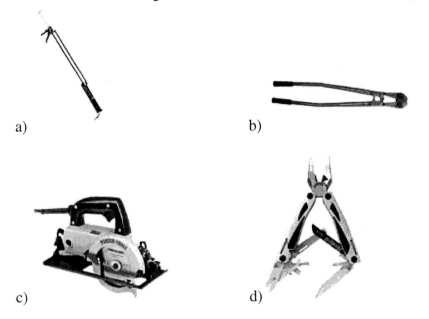

a)

b)

c)

d)

Questions 75 – 77 are based on the following diagram.

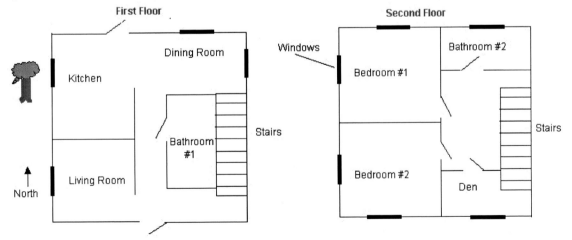

Question 75

What room is directly above the dining room?

a) Bathroom #2

b) Bedroom #2

c) Den

d) Both A and B

Question 76

You are running a hose line and inspecting the outside of the building. Which windows would you be able to see from a position by the tree?

a) Kitchen and Bedroom #1

b) Living room and kitchen

c) Bedroom #1 and Bedroom #2

d) All of the above

Question 77

If the Den is immediately at the top of the stairs, what room would be at the bottom?

a) Front hall

b) Living room

c) Dining room

d) None of the above

Questions 78 – 80 are based on the map below.

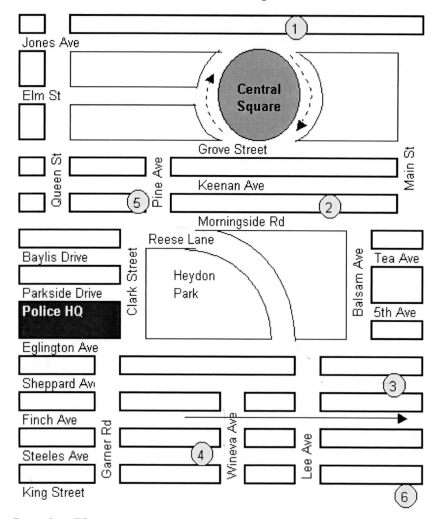

Question 78

There is a stop sign at every single intersection on this map. From position #3, which other Position is reached that involves encountering the fewest number of stop signs?

a) 5　　　　　　　　b) 4　　　　　　　　c) 3　　　　　　　　d) 2

Question 79

Which of the following statements has to be true?

a) Central Square is one-way counter clockwise.

b) Police Headquarters is southwest of Central Square.

c) Finch Avenue runs east one way if Police Headquarters is south of Parkside Drive.

d) Both B and C.

Question 80

Which of the following statements has to be false?

a) Position 5 is east of Position 2.

b) Queen St. is the longest north / south street on the map.

c) Morningside Rd. is the longest north / south street on the map.

d) Garner Rd. runs parallel to Finch Ave.

PROBLEM SOLVING

Question 81

Twenty crates of computers weigh 1 tonne. If each crate weighs 10 kg when empty, how many kilograms of computers are there in one crate?

a) 20   b) 30   c) 40   d) 50

Question 82

Water flows through a damn at a rate of 550 litres in 12 seconds. How much water will flow through in 3 seconds?

a) 120.3 litres   b) 137.5 litres   c) 142.6 litres   d) 183.3 litres

Question 83

Jane ran for 20 minutes at 22 km/h. Then she walked for 10 minutes at 7 km/h and finished up with a light jog at 15 km/h for 30 minutes. Approximately how many kilometres did she cover?

a) 22   b) 16   c) 20   d) 18

Question 84

William wanted to paint his floor. Each litre of paint covers 6 square meters of flooring. How many litres would William need to paint the floor with dimensions measuring 8 meters by 3 meters?

a) 6.5   b) 5   c) 4   d) 3.5

Question 85

Bill and Sue each had a collection of comic books. Bill told Sue, "If you give me 12 of your comic books, I will have twice as many comics as you." Sue made the exact same statement. How many comics did each child have?

a) 30   b) 36   c) 42   d) 48

Question 86

What is the area of the triangle in the diagram below?

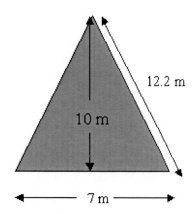

a) 35 metres squared   b) 61 metres squared

c) 42.7 metres squared   d) none of the above

Question 87

What is the area of the shape below?

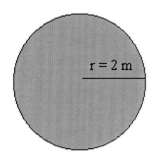

a) 10.2 metres squared

b) 11.5 metres squared

c) 12.6 metres squared

d) 13.2 metres squared

Question 88

What is the volume of the object below?

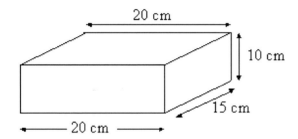

a) 2,000 cm cubed

b) 6,000 cm cubed

c) 4,000 cm cubed

d) none of the above

Question 89

What is 30 divided by 1/2 ?

a) 15   b) 20   c) 30   d) none of these

Question 90

What is two-fifths of a minute?

a) 24 seconds   b) 22 seconds   c) 20 seconds   d) 18 seconds

Question 91

Paulina was painting a picture on a canvas measuring 2 m by 3 m. She has painted 35% of the area. How much area is left that hasn't been painted?

a) 2.7 metres squared

b) 3.5 metres squared

c) 3.9 metres squared

d) 4.3 metres squared

Question 92

Water flows through a pipe at 20,000 cm cubed per second. How many minutes does it take to fill a rectangular tank 3m x 4m x 5m?

a) 65 minutes

b) 50 minutes

c) 20 minutes

d) 10 minutes

Question 93

Natasha worked 8 hours a day, 38 hours a week. She earns $6 an hour. How much will she earn in 3 weeks?

a) $660

b) $684

c) $710

d) $742

Question 94

How many hours will it take a person to walk 10 km at a rate of 3 km/h?

a) 2 1/3 hours

b) 2 2/3 hours

c) 3 1/3 hours

d) none of these

Question 95

Simon studied longer than Shelley, but not as long as Kate. Shelley did all of her studying with Claire. Claire then studied with Kate. Who did the least studying?

a) Kate

b) Claire

c) Simon

d) Shelley

Question 96

A floor in a warehouse has a width of 15 metres and a length of 30 metres. There is a circular carpet on the floor with a radius of 1 metre. What is the area of the floor that is not covered by the carpet?

a) 221.86 square metres

b) 86.86 square metres

c) 446.86 square metres

d) none of the above

Question 97

A firefighter needs to cover the area described below with a square tarp. What is the area of the smallest square tarp that will fully cover the area below?

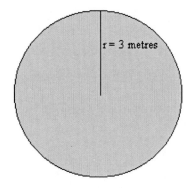

r = 3 metres

a) 36 square metres   b) 30 square metres   c) 24 square metres   d) 20 square metres

Question 98

In a pizza eating contest a man can eat an eighth of his own weight in 45 minutes. If the man weighs 80 kg, how much can he eat in 30 minutes?

a) 5 1/3 kg   b) 5 2/3 kg   c) 6 1/3 kg   d) 6 2/3 kg

Question 99

For the past week John jogged every day and increased his distance by 1.5 km every day. Last Tuesday, John ran 2 km but today he ran 6.5 km. What day of the week is it today?

a) Friday   b) Thursday   c) Sunday   d) Saturday

Question 100

How much effort is required to lift a 4000 kg vehicle using a jackscrew with a 40 cm handle and a 1/3 cm screw pitch?

a) 10.7 kg   b) 8.1 kg   c) 5.3 kg   d) none of these

Memory	
1)	A
2)	C
3)	D
4)	B
5)	B
6)	D
7)	A
8)	A
9)	D
10)	B
11)	C
12)	A
13)	C
14)	D
15)	A
16)	C
17)	B
18)	B
19)	A
20)	C

Reading Comp	
21)	B
22)	A
23)	C
24)	A
25)	D
26)	D
27)	B
28)	C
29)	A
30)	C
31)	D
32)	C
33)	B
34)	A
35)	D
36)	D
37)	B
38)	D
39)	A
40)	B

Work Relations	
41)	C
42)	A
43)	D
44)	B
45)	B
46)	B
47)	A
48)	C
49)	A
50)	D
51)	C
52)	A
53)	B
54)	C
55)	D
56)	A
57)	C
58)	D
59)	B
60)	B

Mechanical Apt.	
61)	A
62)	C
63)	A
64)	B
65)	B
66)	D
67)	A
68)	C
69)	A
70)	B
71)	C
72)	D
73)	C
74)	B
75)	A
76)	D
77)	C
78)	A
79)	C
80)	D

Mathematics	
81)	C
82)	B
83)	B
84)	C
85)	B
86)	A
87)	C
88)	D
89)	D
90)	A
91)	C
92)	B
93)	B
94)	C
95)	D
96)	C
97)	A
98)	D
99)	A
100)	C

Question 41

C - Let James know that jokes like that are inappropriate, and inform a supervisor.

Racist jokes are inappropriate and should be brought to the immediate attention of a supervisor. Option A will make Dave feel that he is alone in this situation. Options B and D fail to address the situation of racist jokes occurring at the work place.

Question 42

A - Apologize to the owner and ask him where you should place the chair.

It is important to realize that victims of fire are most often upset with the situation rather than the individual firefighter. Option B is inappropriate, as you have no idea how important the chair is to the owner. Options C and D are inappropriate, as they fail to address the immediate concern of the owner. They may also escalate the situation. There is nothing wrong with apologizing to the owner and attempting to help him as much as possible.

Question 43

D - Perform CPR without the proper equipment despite the fact that you feel you are putting yourself at risk of contracting a communicable disease. This man needs help.

This is often a tricky situation. In an emergency situation, you may be required to risk your life, but at the same time you have the proper equipment and take every measure to protect yourself. If you feel that there is a serious threat of acquiring a communicable disease through CPR, you are well within your rights not to perform the act. Make sure that you immediately get help on the way for the man.

Question 44

B - Do nothing. This situation doesn't directly affect you and should be handled by those personally involved.

There are bound to be problems such as this when firefighters work together closely. This situation doesn't affect you at all. Option A is inappropriate because the people affected can speak to a supervisor if they wish. Option C is inappropriate as you are not the supervisor in charge of the station. Option D would also be inappropriate as talking behind peoples' backs creates a poor work environment.

Question 45

B - Pull Peter privately aside and ask him to lay off with the jokes.

Option A could lead to an open confrontation involving your entire shift. Option C is also inappropriate as it fails to address the problem. It may also create more tension between you and Peter. Option D is a possibility that you could use only after discussing the situation with Peter privately.

Question 46

B - Inform your supervisor about the situation. Behaviour like that is inexcusable in emergency situations and has to be reported.

Option A fails to address the situation and is, therefore, inappropriate. Option C is inadequate as Charles put lives in danger with his behaviour. Option D involves talking behind the backs of co-workers. This is never a way to resolve problems.

Question 47

A - Place your mask on and use the air supply to prevent yourself from breathing dangerous fumes while completing your work.

Option A would be inappropriate as you are not their supervisor and they are senior to you. Option C is inappropriate because you feel there is a health risk to not wearing a mask. Peer pressure can be difficult to overcome, but your health is more important. Leaving the apartment is not an option, as you have work to perform there.

Question 48

C - Being under the influence of an illegal drug while on duty is the most serious offence.

Although all of the options are serious offences, Option C would be the most serious. You are putting your co-workers at a great deal of risk with this type of behaviour.

Question 49

A - Approach the two parties to attempt to separate them and diffuse the situation.

Option B is not the best option. Siding immediately with your co-worker without understanding the situation appears completely biased, and may negate any ability to diffuse the situation. Option C is not appropriate as the heated verbal altercation is evidence that your co-worker may need assistance. Option D is also inappropriate because you shouldn't make rash decisions unless you have more information about what started the problem. Disciplining a co-worker in public is also inappropriate.

Question 50

D - Both B and C.

This question asks for the inappropriate actions in this situation. There is nothing wrong with supporting friends and family members when they are applying for a job. Firefighting is a difficult career to enter and excellent candidates will need support. However, providing support to which others do not have access to is inappropriate and shouldn't be done. This would include providing a copy of the application test

Question 51

C - Pull Sean aside to let him know how you saw it, and tell him that you will have to inform the officer of what you saw.

Options A and B are dishonest and illegal. Lying to supervisors, or investigators, is completely inappropriate behaviour for a firefighter. You will not have a choice as to whether you will give a statement to the officer or not (Option D). One thing to consider in these situations are civilian witnesses. If firefighters state that the light was green, yet there are several civilian witnesses who state that it was red, this could reflect poorly on the fire department.

Question 52

A - Call other firefighters for assistance.

Firefighting is dependant on teamwork. Options B and C demonstrate that you are unwilling to work with people to solve problems. Fire departments don't want to hire people who think they can handle situations completely on their own and don't need the assistance of others. A fire is a very dangerous situation. Waiting for things to change and hoping for the best (Option D) is also inappropriate.

Question 53

B - Pick up the man and immediately get him to safety.

It is important to respect the wishes of the public while interacting with them. However, this is an emergency situation and the man is in hysterics. Your number one priority is getting him and others to safety. This is why Options A and D are inappropriate. Option C is likewise inappropriate because fellow firefighters have more pressing concerns at this stage than salvaging furniture.

Question 54

C - Order the firefighter to continue into the building with the original team.

This question asks for the inappropriate action to take in this situation. Both A and C are appropriate actions. The safety of the firefighter and the team are paramount. Entering a burning building with an injured party would be inappropriate (Option C).

Question 55

D - All of the above.

Bribery is a very serious offence. In this case you should continue with the fines as you planned, caution the superintendent against bribery and inform your supervisor. Failing to take all three of these measures may result in more bribery attempts. Charging the male with a crime is another option that was not presented.

Question 56

A - Inform your captain that you are too ill to continue duties and book off sick.

Options B and C are inappropriate responses because they may put the lives of yourself and co-workers in danger in an emergency situation. Option D is also inappropriate. The reason you are at work is to be ready in case you are needed for an emergency. If you are not prepared to handle an emergency situation, you should not be at work. Booking off sick will allow your captain to arrange a replacement.

Question 57

C - Notify your captain of the situation and your suspicion.

There is no reason why informing your captain would hinder a police investigation (Option A). Options B and D would be inappropriate as the watches do not belong to you and you have no right to take them.

Question 58

D - Either A or C would be acceptable.

It would be completely inappropriate to show up late for work without informing your captain on the presumption that he wouldn't mind (Option B). Because you are required for work, leaving the charity would be justifiable in this situation (Option A). Option C would also be appropriate as your captain may be able to arrange someone to cover for you for half an hour.

Question 59

B - Report the incident to your captain.

Option A is not appropriate because sabotaging equipment is a very dangerous situation and should never be tolerated. Option C would not treat the situation with the seriousness that it deserves. Option D would also fail to address the problem. If sabotage did occur, and you had done nothing, Grant's life, or those of other firefighters, could be placed in jeopardy.

Question 60

B - Immediately inform your supervisor and other firefighters.

Firefighting is a team project. It is vital that your co-workers are immediately made aware of any potential dangers. Options A, B and C would place your co-workers at risk as they would not be aware of what you know. Information sharing is of paramount importance in these situations.

Question 61

First determine the circumference of the arc that the screw handle will make.

$$c = 2 (\pi) (r)$$
$$= 2 (3.14) (30)$$
$$= 6.28 (30)$$
$$= 188.4 \text{ cm}$$

Now determine the mechanical advantage that the jackscrew provides.

M.A. = circumference / screw pitch
$$= 188.4 \div 1/3 \quad \text{When dividing fractions, you have to multiply by the}$$
$$= 188.4 \times 3 \quad \text{reciprocal.}$$
$$= 565.2$$

Finally, calculate the resistance or weight that can be lifted.

Resistance = M.A. x effort
$$= 565.2 \times 10$$
$$= 5,652 \text{ kg}$$

Question 62

This is an example of a second-class lever. The closer the material being lifted is to the pivot point, or fulcrum, the easier the lift will be. If box B is moved closer to box A, the lift will be easier. However, the potential height the box can be lifted will be sacrificed.

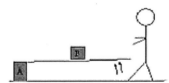

Question 63

Because the larger wheel is three times the size of the smaller one, every time the larger wheel makes one complete revolution the smaller wheel has to make three. To determine the speed of the smaller wheel, simply multiply by 3 times the number of revolutions the larger wheel has per minute.

$$3 \times 600 = 1,800 \text{ rpm}$$

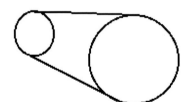

Question 64

Gears will respond the same way as belt drives when larger and smaller gears are placed together. Every time gear B makes one complete revolution, gears A and C will not make a complete turn. Therefore, gear B has to have a higher rpm than the other two gears. Size of gears and the number of teeth gears have will affect the rpm.

Question 65

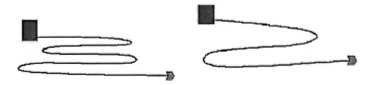

The transport of water loses efficiency in this case by two factors:

1) The length of the hose.
2) The number of creases, which force the water to change direction.

The correct choice is the layout with the fewest number of creases.

Question 66

One of the best ways to answer this problem is to determine which gears will turn the same way. Any two gears touching will spin in opposite directions.

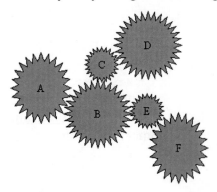

Group 1	Group 2
A	B
C	D
E	F

Question 75

Question 76

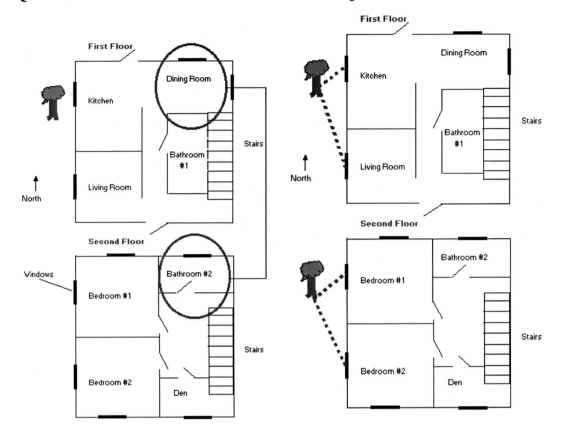

Question 77

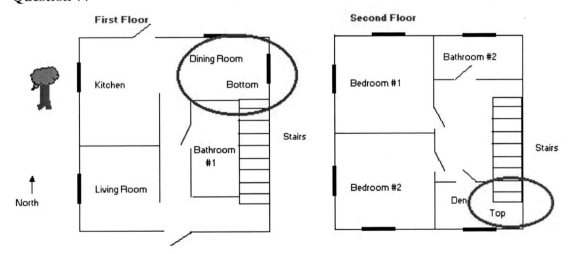

Question 78

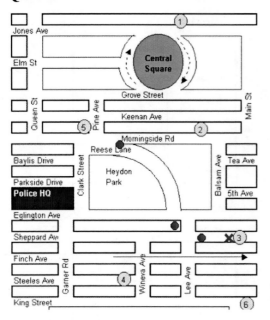

There would be three stop signs while traveling to location 5.

Question 79

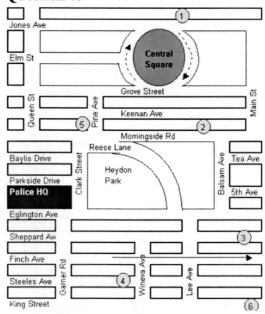

If Police HQ is south of Parkside Dr., that makes North would be this direction. Finch would therefore be one-way east.

Question 80

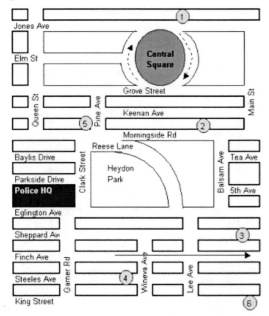

In order to run parallel, both streets would have to be running in the same direction and never meet. Because they meet at 90-degree angles they are perpendicular rather than parallel.

Question 81

First determine how much the crate weighs with the computers. Divide the total weight (1 tonne) by the number of crates (20). There are 1,000 kg in a tonne.

1000 / 20 = 50   Therefore, each crate with computers weighs 50 kg.

Take the weight of each crate (10 kg) from the total weight of a crate and a computer (50 kg).

50 – 10 = 40 kg

Question 82

First you must set up an algebraic equation. In 12 seconds, 550 litres will flow. Assuming that the same proportion of water will flow, establish a relationship between the time and the water flow.

$$\frac{3}{12} = \frac{y}{550}$$ 3/12 is equal to 1/4. This will make the calculation easier.

$$\frac{1}{4} = \frac{y}{550}$$ You must isolate "y" by multiplying both sides of the equation by 550.

$$\frac{550}{4} = y$$ 550 / 4 = 137.5 litres

Question 83

Start by solving how far she ran in the first 20 minutes. Because she was running 22 km / hour, and she ran for 20 / 60 of an hour, simply multiply the speed and the times together for the distance.

Distance 1
$$\frac{20}{60} \times 22 = 7.3 \text{ km}$$

Distance 2
$$\frac{10}{60} \times 7 = 1.2 \text{ km}$$

Distance 3
$$\frac{30}{60} \times 15 = 7.5 \text{ km}$$

Finally, add up all of the distances (7.3 + 1.2 + 7.5 = 16 km).

Question 84

The area of the floor is 24 square meters (8 x 3). Therefore, it will take 4 litres of paint to cover the floor (24 / 6 = 4).

Question 85

This question will require an algebraic equation. "Y" represents the number of comic books that both children have. If we increase "y" by 12, then it must equal twice the number of "y" – 12. The equation would be written:

$$y + 12 = 2(y - 12)$$
Brackets have to be handled first. Multiply 2 to both "y" and 12.

$$y + 12 = 2y - 24$$
Collect like terms by subtracting "y" from both sides.

$$12 = 2y - y - 24$$
Followed by adding 24 to both sides.

$$12 + 24 = 2y - y$$
This will work out to: $36 = y$

Because "y" represents the number of comic books that each child has, each child has 36 comic books.

Question 86

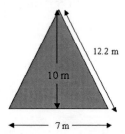

The formula for the area of a triangle is:

A = 1/2 x base x height
= 1/2 x 7 x 10
= 1/2 x 70
= 35 m²

Question 87

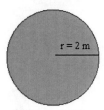

The area of a circle is calculated through the following formula:

a = π r²
= 3.14 x 2²
= 3.14 (4)   Remember order of operation.
= 12.6 m²

Question 88

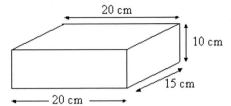

To calculate the volume of a cube, use the formula below:

$$V = (l) \times (w) \times (h)$$
$$= 20 \times 15 \times 10$$
$$= 300 \times 10$$
$$= 3,000 \text{ m}^3$$

Question 89

When you divide by a fraction, you have to multiply one number by the reciprocal.

$30 \div 1/2$ becomes $30 \times 2/1$ or $30 \times 2 = 60$

Question 90

In order to calculate 2/5 of a minute, multiply 2/5 x 60.

$2/5 \times 60 = 120 / 5 = 24$ seconds.

Question 91

First determine the total area of the canvas by multiplying the dimensions 2 m x 3 m = 6 metres squared.

Next determine how much of the canvas has already been painted. Multiply the area (6) times the percent painted (35% or 0.35).

$6 \times 0.35 = 2.1$ square metres

Finally, subtract the amount painted from the total area of the canvas to determine what remains to be painted.

$6 - 2.1 = 3.9$ square metres

Question 92

First calculate the total volume of the tank in cubic cm. Remember there are 100 cm in a metre.

Volume = length x width x height
= 300 x 400 x 500 = 60,000,000 cubic cm

Next determine the number of seconds that it will take to fill the tank. This is accomplished by dividing the volume by the rate the water is flowing.

6,000,000 / 20,000 = 3,000 seconds

Finally, convert the number of seconds to minutes. Since there are 60 seconds in a minute, by dividing 3,000 by 60 you will arrive at a time in minutes.

3,000 / 60 = 50 minutes

Question 93

First determine how much money is made in one week.

38 x $6 = $228

Then multiply the number of weeks by how much she earns next week.

$228 x 3 = $684

Question 94

Divide the total distance to be covered by the rate of speed.

10 / 3 = 3.33 hours to walk 10 km at a rate of 3 km per hour.

0.33 = 1/3, so the total is 3 1/3 hours.

Question 95

This problem requires an ordering of information.

First Sentence: Kate
                       Simon
                       Shelley

Second Sentence: Shelley = Clair

Third Sentence: Claire does more studying than Shelley.

Therefore, Shelley does the least amount of studying.

Question 96

First determine the area of the entire floor.

$$\text{area} = \text{length x width}$$
$$= 30 \times 15$$
$$= 450 \text{ m}^2$$

Next determine the area of the rug on the floor.

$$\text{area} = \pi r^2$$
$$= 3.14 \times 1^2$$
$$= 3.14 \text{ m}^2$$

Finally, subtract the area the carpet is covering from the area of the entire floor.

$$450 - 3.14 = 446.86 \text{ m}^2$$

Question 97

The diameter of the circle above is 6 metres (2 x radius). This is how long each side of the square has to be in order to fully cover the area of the circle. Follow the formula for area of a square to answer the question.

$$A = (1) \times (w)$$
$$= (6) \times (6)$$
$$= 36 \text{ m}^2$$

There will be excess material in this scenario, represented by the diagram above.

Question 98

First determine how many kilograms he can eat in 45 minutes. To calculate 1/8 of 80 kgs, divide 80 by 8.

$$80 / 8 = 10 \text{ kg}$$

To determine how much he can eat in 30 minutes (2/3 of 45 minutes) multiply 2/3 and 10 kg.

$$10 \times 2/3 = 20/3$$

By dividing 20 by 3 you will end up with 6.66, which is 6 2/3 kg.

Question 99

First determine the number of kilometres by which John has increased his distance.

$$6.5 - 2 = 4.5 \text{ km}$$

Now divide the increased number of km (4.5) by the number that John increases by each day (1.5).

$$4.5 / 1.5 = 3 \text{ days have elapsed since John ran 2 km on Tuesday.}$$

0	1	2	3
Tuesday	Wednesday	Thursday	Friday

Question 100

First determine the circumference of the arc that the screw handle will make.

$$
\begin{aligned}
c &= 2\,(\pi)\,(r) \\
&= 2\,(3.14)\,(40) \\
&= 6.28\,(40) \\
&= 251.2 \text{ cm}
\end{aligned}
$$

Next determine the mechanical advantage that the jackscrew provides.

$$
\begin{aligned}
\text{M.A.} &= \text{circumference / screw pitch} \\
&= 251.2 \div 1/3 \\
&= 251.2 \times 3 \\
&= 753.6
\end{aligned}
$$

Finally, manipulate the equation to work out the effort required, given the resistance.

$$
\begin{aligned}
\text{Resistance} &= \text{M.A.} \times \text{effort} \\
4{,}000 &= 753.6 \times \text{effort} \\
4{,}000 / 753.6 &= \text{effort} \qquad \text{(divide both sides by 753.6 to isolate effort)} \\
\text{effort} &= 5.3 \text{ kg}
\end{aligned}
$$

This practice tests contains several different components, including confidence metrics, psychological testing, arithmetic questions, mechanical aptitude questions and judgment questions. On the answer sheet, fill in the letter corresponding to the correct answer for the appropriate questions. For questions requiring a choice between 1 and 9, fill in the appropriate number in the space provided.

The only materials you can use during the test are a pencil and scrap paper. No calculators, books or counting devices are permitted. Give yourself one hour to complete the exam.

	A B C D		A B C D						A B C D		
1)	○○○○	2)	○○○○	3)	____	4)	____	5)	○○○○	6)	_____
7)	○○○○	8)	○○○○	9)	____	10)	____	11)	○○○○	12)	_____
13)	○○○○	14)	○○○○	15)	____	16)	____	17)	○○○○	18)	_____
19)	○○○○	20)	○○○○	21)	____	22)	____	23)	○○○○	24)	_____
25)	○○○○	26)	○○○○	27)	____	28)	____	29)	○○○○	30)	_____
31)	○○○○	32)	○○○○	33)	____	34)	____	35)	○○○○	36)	_____
37)	○○○○	38)	○○○○	39)	____	40)	____	41)	○○○○	42)	_____
43)	○○○○	44)	○○○○	45)	____	46)	____	47)	○○○○	48)	_____
49)	○○○○	50)	○○○○	51)	____	52)	____	53)	○○○○	54)	_____
55)	○○○○	56)	○○○○	57)	____	58)	____	59)	○○○○	60)	_____
61)	○○○○	62)	○○○○	63)	____	64)	____	65)	○○○○	66)	_____
67)	○○○○	68)	○○○○	69)	____	70)	____	71)	○○○○	72)	_____
73)	○○○○	74)	○○○○	75)	____	76)	____	77)	○○○○	78)	_____
79)	○○○○	80)	○○○○	81)	____	82)	____	83)	○○○○	84)	_____
85)	○○○○	86)	○○○○	87)	____	88)	____	89)	○○○○	90)	_____
91)	○○○○	92)	○○○○	93)	____	94)	____	95)	○○○○	96)	_____
97)	○○○○	98)	○○○○	99)	____	100)	____	101)	○○○○	102)	_____
103)	○○○○	104)	○○○○	105)	____	106)	____	107)	○○○○	108)	_____
109)	○○○○	110)	○○○○	111)	____	112)	____	113)	○○○○	114)	_____
115)	○○○○	116)	○○○○	117)	____	118)	____	119)	○○○○	120)	_____
121)	○○○○	122)	○○○○	123)	____	124)	____	125)	○○○○		

____ / 21   ____ / 21   ____ / 21

Question 1

Paulina was painting a picture on a canvas measuring 3m by 5 m. She has painted 2/5's of the area. How much area is left that hasn't been painted?

a) 7 m²   b) 8 m²

c) 9 m²   d) 10 m²

Question 2

You take your children on a tour of the firehall at which you work. Which of the following actions would be unacceptable?

a) Take them upstairs to the private living area.

b) Allow them to slide down the pole.

c) Remove equipment from the truck for them to play with.

d) All of the above.

Question 3

While responding to a medical complaint you are required to work on a 35-year-old woman who is having an epileptic fit. She is on the ground shaking very badly and blood is trickling from her mouth. On a scale of 1 to 9, with 9 being the most severe, how distraught would you be?

                1   2   4   5   6   7   8   9

Not distraught at all   Extremely distraught

Question 4

On a scale of 1 to 9, with 9 being unable to perform your duties, how would the above situation affect your job performance?

                1   2   4   5   6   7   8   9

No Affect   Unable to Perform Duties

Question 5

You are dispatched to a fire in progress. While enroute you drive by a schoolyard. It is 3:00 pm and the school has just let out. Which of the following is the most appropriate action?

a) Continue to the fire call, and disregard the children in the area.

b) Take a different route to the fire to avoid passing the schoolyard, even though it is longer.

c) Slow the truck down and drive with more caution when pass the schoolyard.

d) Turn off your lights and sirens so children will not be attracted to the fire truck.

Question 6

How confident are you with the decision you made above on a scale of 1 to 9, with 9 being the most confident?

	1	2	4	5	6	7	8	9

Not Confident   Moderately Confident   Extremely Confident

Question 7

What tool would you use to determine a vertical line?

a) Micrometer callipers   b) Tape measure

c) Plumb bob   d) Voltmeter

Question 8

Captain Gordon handed you a multi-purpose tool while you were working on a fire. During the fire you lost the tool and afterward forgot about it. Two weeks later, Captain Gordon complains that he can't remember where he left his tool. Which of the following actions is acceptable?

a) Purchase Captain Gordon a new multi-purpose tool as it was your fault it was lost.

b) Disregard the situation because it was not your fault the tool was lost. These things occasionally happen during fires.

c) Tell Captain Gordon what happened to the tool.

d) Either A or C would be acceptable.

Question 9

While on vacation, you witness a 25-year-old woman get pulled under water in the ocean. You assist the lifeguards as they pull her to safety. She is not breathing when she is laid on the beach. On a scale of 1 to 9, with 9 being the most severe, how distraught would you be?

	1	2	4	5	6	7	8	9

Not distraught at all   Extremely distraught

Question 10

On a scale of 1 to 9, with 9 being unable to perform your duties, how would the above situation affect your job performance?

	1	2	4	5	6	7	8	9

No Affect   Unable to Perform Duties

Question 11

You are attending a medical complaint of a baby that was left in the car on a hot summer day. When you arrive at the mall parking lot you can see an unconscious baby in the back seat of the car. It must be well over 100 degrees Fahrenheit inside. You have to get the baby out immediately. In which order would you perform the following options?

        A - Break the glass.

        B - Page the mother in the mall.

        C - Call a tow truck to bring a lock pick to unlock the door.

        D - Check to see if the door is open.

        E - Use a power saw to cut through the roof.

a) D, A, C, E, B

b) A, D, E, C, B

c) D, B, A, C, E

d) B, D, A, C, E

Question 12

How confident are you with the decision you made above on a scale of 1 to 9, with 9 being the most confident?

       1   2   4   5   6   7   8   9

Not Confident   Moderately Confident   Extremely Confident

Question 13

In order to raise a 150 kg barrel to a 3-metre elevation, you will use a 12 metre ramp. How much effort is required to roll the barrel up the ramp?

a) 32.1 kg

b) 37.5 kg

c) 41.8 kg

d) 45.2 kg

Question 14

As a firefighter you notice one of your co-workers constantly placing equipment in the wrong location. What would be the best way to handle this situation?

a) Immediately report the errors to a supervisor so he can correct the problem.

b) Mention this poor performance to your other co-workers.

c) Advise your co-worker on the proper placement of the equipment and inform a supervisor only if the problem persists.

d) Chastise the co-worker for poor performance on the job.

Question 15

While returning to the station after a medical complaint one of your co-workers begins to suffer a heart attack. He is transported to the hospital, but is later pronounced dead. On a scale of 1 to 9, with 9 being the most severe, how distraught would you be?

       1   2   4   5   6   7   8   9

Not distraught at all   Extremely distraught

Question 16

On a scale of 1 to 9, with 9 being unable to perform your duties, how would the above situation affect your job performance?

           1   2   4   5   6   7   8   9

No Affect   Unable to Perform Duties

Question 17

When you arrive at a medical complaint for a collapse you see a woman lying unconscious on the kitchen floor. There is a toaster plugged into the wall that is hissing and emitting electrical sparks. Which of the following actions should you take first?

a) Check to see if the woman is breathing.

b) Unplug the toaster.

c) Use a type C fire extinguisher on the toaster (safe for electrical fires).

d) Remove the woman from the area.

Question 18

How confident are you with the decision you made above on a scale of 1 to 9, with 9 being the most confident?

           1   2   4   5   6   7   8   9

Not Confident   Moderately Confident   Extremely Confident

Question 19

What is 25% of 1 hour and 45 minutes?

a) 28 minutes and 15 seconds   b) 27 minutes and 25 seconds

c) 26 minutes and 25 seconds   d) 26 minutes and 15 seconds

Question 20

Lance, one of your fellow firefighters is hurt in a fire and rushed to hospital. After the fire is extinguished you notice Lance's equipment discarded by the truck. There is a money clip by the equipment that doesn't contain any identification. What action is most appropriate?

a) Collect the money and bring it to Lance, as it appears to be his.

b) Collect the money for Lance and, if he says it is not his, then inform your captain.

c) Inform your captain about what you found and where it was found.

d) Either B or C would be appropriate.

Question 21

While fighting a fire you lose track of your team and, as a result, one of your co-workers gets trapped in a burning building. He receives some minor burns in the fire. On a scale of 1 to 9, with 9 being the most severe, how distraught would you be?

    1   2   4   5   6   7   8   9
Not distraught at all   Extremely distraught

Question 22

On a scale of 1 to 9, with 9 being unable to perform your duties, how would the above situation affect your job performance?

    1   2   4   5   6   7   8   9
No Affect   Unable to Perform Duties

Question 23

Firefighters often have to break down doors to gain access to victims and property during fires. Which of the following is not an important consideration a firefighter should make before attempting to break down a door?

a) Check for smoke around the door.

b) Feel the door for heat.

c) Stand to the side of the door before breaking it open.

d) None of the above.

Question 24

How confident are you with the decision you made above on a scale of 1 to 9, with 9 being the most confident?

    1   2   4   5   6   7   8   9
Not Confident   Moderately Confident   Extremely Confident

Question 25

If a crow bar is used to lift a heavy box, as shown in the diagram below, how much weight could be lifted with the 15 kg of effort?

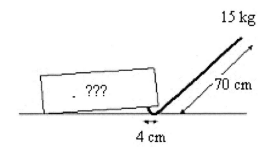

a) 262.5 kg   b) 258.3 kg

c) 252.2 kg   d) 246.5 kg

Question 26

While off duty, you witness a severe auto accident. There is a police officer on the scene who appears to be alone and needs help with the multiple people injured. Which of the following actions would be most appropriate?

a) Continue driving on as the officer probably has back-up enroute and you would only get in the way.

b) Approach the officer, identify yourself and ask if she needs assistance.

c) As you continue driving on, call 911 and advise that the officer needs more assistance.

d) Stop your vehicle and take control of the scene, as you have more medical training than the officer.

Question 27

While at a fire scene you encounter a small child who is trapped under some debris. The area has to be vacated immediately. However, moving the child causes extreme pain to her. On a scale of 1 to 9, with 9 being the most severe, how distraught would you be?

	1	2	4	5	6	7	8	9

Not distraught at all   Extremely distraught

Question 28

On a scale of 1 to 9, with 9 being unable to perform your duties, how would the above situation affect your job performance?

	1	2	4	5	6	7	8	9

No Affect   Unable to Perform Duties

Question 29

While going to work you witness a motor vehicle accident. Both cars are smoking and a fire breaks out. Two of the people involved stumble a safe distance from the burning vehicles, but the driver of one car is unconscious behind the wheel. Gasoline is leaking from one of the vehicles. In what order would you take the following steps?

    A - Grab your small portable fire extinguisher from your trunk.

    B - Attempt to drag the driver out of the car.

    C - Call 911 on your cell phone.

    D - Keep a safe distance from the vehicles.

    E - Do nothing and wait for emergency personnel.

a) B, D, C, E   b) A, B, E, D

c) C, D, E, B   d) C, D, E, A

Question 30

How confident are you with the decision you made above on a scale of 1 to 9, with 9 being the most confident?

	1	2	4	5	6	7	8	9

Not Confident   Moderately Confident   Extremely Confident

Question 31

A floor in a warehouse has a width of 25 metres and a length of 40 metres. There are three circular vents on the floor with a diameter of 4 metres each. What is the area of the floor that does not include the vents?

a) 912.38 m² b) 943.72 m²

c) 962.32 m² d) none of the above

Question 32

While at a party you are approached by a friend who works as a reporter for a newspaper. He begins asking questions about a co-worker of yours who is being charged with arson. As you worked closely with this firefighter, you are quite involved in the investigation. What is the best course of action?

a) Inform your friend that you can't talk about the situation and advise him to contact media relations if he needs more information.

b) Answer any questions you feel are appropriate as no one ordered you not to speak to the press.

c) Talk to the reporter solely off the record.

d) Accuse the reporter of taking advantage of your friendship and leave the party.

Question 33

While fighting a fire in an apartment building you encounter a victim who has been struck on the head with fallen debris. The victim is shaking badly and appears to be having an uncontrollable fit and going into shock. On a scale of 1 to 9, with 9 being the most severe, how distraught would you be?

	1	2	4	5	6	7	8	9

Not distraught at all   Extremely distraught

Question 34

On a scale of 1 to 9, with 9 being unable to perform your duties, how would the above situation affect your job performance?

	1	2	4	5	6	7	8	9

No Affect   Unable to Perform Duties

Question 35

While fighting a house fire you find an unconscious dog in the bedroom. The entire house is engulfed in flame. In which order would perform the following options?

       A – Remove the dog from the building.

       B – Check to see if the dog was alive.

       C – Call for assistance to remove the dog.

       D – Disregard the dog and continue fighting the fire.

a) A, B   b) C, D

c) B, C   d) D

Question 36

How confident are you with the decision you made above on a scale of 1 to 9, with 9 being the most confident?

1	2	4	5	6	7	8	9

Not Confident   Moderately Confident   Extremely Confident

Question 37

Solve for "Y" $2 (Y + 15) - 75 = 225$

a) 120   b) 125

c) 130   d) 135

Question 38

You are dispatched to a medical complaint. As you arrive on the scene you see a large group of youths tending to an unconscious female. One of the youths approaches you screaming that you took too long to arrive. What action should you take?

a) Talk to the youth and explain that you were only dispatched 5 minutes ago.

b) Begin the formal process of handling a complaint.

c) Ignore the youth and tend to the unconscious female immediately.

d) Tell the youth to talk to your captain and point out whom he is.

Question 39

While responding to an industrial accident at a water plant you are required to pull a victim from a water purification tank into which he has accidentally fallen. The man was trapped for several minutes and is now not breathing. On a scale of 1 to 9, with 9 being the most severe, how distraught would you be?

1	2	4	5	6	7	8	9

Not distraught at all   Extremely distraught

Question 40

On a scale of 1 to 9, with 9 being unable to perform your duties, how would the above situation affect your job performance?

          1   2   4   5   6   7   8   9
No Affect   Unable to Perform Duties

Question 41

Which of the following statements about electrical fires is true?

a) They can be effectively put out with water.

b) They are extinguished by removing the source of electrical power.

c) They can only be extinguished through smothering the flame.

d) None of the above.

Question 42

How confident are you with the decision you made above on a scale of 1 to 9, with 9 being the most confident?

          1   2   4   5   6   7   8   9
 Not Confident   Moderately Confident   Extremely Confident

Question 43

Which of the following statements best describes what this tool is commonly used for?

a) Adjustable tool most often used for tightening or loosening bolts.

b) Adjustable tool used to grip round objects such as steel rods or pipes.

c) Used to secure a wood or metal work piece while work is performed.

d) Cuts metal pipe by continually circling the pipe and increasing the torque.

Question 44

You are a new recruit on the shift and hear several of your co-workers arranging to have a cake brought in for your captain, who is celebrating his birthday. They plan to surprise the captain with his favourite meal for dinner tomorrow evening. What course of action is most appropriate?

a) Ignore the situation and let events unfold without interference.

b) Approach your co-workers and offer to assist in the preparation.

c) Neither A nor B would be inappropriate behaviour because the firefighters would not be violating any procedures.

d) Neither A nor B would be appropriate, as the captain should know of all matters in the station.

Question 45

You are on the scene of a male who committed suicide by jumping from a bridge. The man was carrying his 7-year-old son with him when he jumped. Both males are dead. On a scale of 1 to 9, with 9 being the most severe, how distraught would you be?

          1   2   4   5   6   7   8   9

Not distraught at all   Extremely distraught

Question 46

On a scale of 1 to 9, with 9 being unable to perform your duties, how would the above situation affect your job performance?

          1   2   4   5   6   7   8   9

No Affect   Unable to Perform Duties

Question 47

While responding to a medical complaint in a park you encounter a man lying unconscious. His friend says he collapsed for no reason. As your co-workers begin working on the male, you discover several hypodermic needles lying nearby. Which of the following are appropriate steps to take?

a) Immediately inform your co-workers of the needles.

b) Search the area for more needles or drug paraphernalia.

c) Ask the victim's friend about the type of drugs used.

d) All of the above.

Question 48

How confident are you with the decision you made above on a scale of 1 to 9, with 9 being the most confident?

          1   2   4   5   6   7   8   9

Not Confident   Moderately Confident   Extremely Confident

Question 49

Which of the following statements is true based on the picture below?

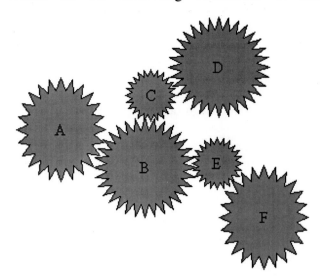

a) Gears A, C and F will all turn in the same direction.

b) Gears C and E will have a faster rpm speed than gear B.

c) If gear A turns clockwise, so will gears C, E, and F.

d) Gears A, B and D will spin at the same speed.

Question 50

A woman runs into the fire station and informs you that there is a fire in a house down the street. You should:

a) Inform your supervisor immediately.

b) Take down the female's name, address and other relevant information.

c) Head to the house so you can determine whether her information is legitimate.

d) Tell her to call 911 immediately so that you can officially be dispatched.

Question 51

While attempting to extricate a victim from a motor vehicle collision you misjudge the depth of the saw blade and accidentally cut one of the victim's arms. On a scale of 1 to 9, with 9 being the most severe, how distraught would you be?

1	2	4	5	6	7	8	9

Not distraught at all   Extremely distraught

Question 52

On a scale of 1 to 9, with 9 being unable to perform your duties, how would the above situation affect your job performance?

1	2	4	5	6	7	8	9

No Affect   Unable to Perform Duties

Question 53

You are dispatched to a medical complaint of a woman who states she fell down the stairs. When you arrive you are confronted by a man with a gun who says you cannot enter his house and treat his wife. He slams the door shut. Which of the following options would you choose to do?

a) Knock on the door and ask to speak to the wife.

b) Rush into the house with your axe, as the woman needs immediate assistance.

c) Call the police immediately.

d) Both B and C.

Question 54

How confident are you with the decision you made above on a scale of 1 to 9, with 9 being the most confident?

          1   2   4   5   6   7   8   9
 Not Confident   Moderately Confident   Extremely Confident

Question 55

There are three pizzas, which were completely eaten by four groups. One pizza had 18 slices, another had 1.5 times that many slices, and the largest had even three more slices than that. Group A ate 1/3 of the slices. Group B ate 40% of the slices. If Group D ate only ½ as much as Group C, how many slices did Group D eat?

a) 6.7   b) 10

c) 5   d) 8.3

Question 56

After extinguishing a small kitchen fire in a first floor apartment you come across a diary lying upside down on a stand in one of the bedrooms. Which of the following actions would be appropriate?

a) Take the diary to your captain.

b) Inspect the diary to see if there are clues to the cause of the fire.

c) Ignore the diary.

d) Glance through the diary to see who it belongs to.

Question 57

Your son is injured in a fire caused by the barbeque. He is in a tremendous amount of pain due to a third-degree burn on his left arm. You are unable to do anything to ease the pain as you transport him to the hospital. On a scale of 1 to 9, with 9 being the most severe, how distraught would you be?

          1   2   4   5   6   7   8   9
 Not distraught at all   Extremely distraught

Question 58

On a scale of 1 to 9, with 9 being unable to perform your duties, how would the above situation affect your job performance?

    1   2   4   5   6   7   8   9

No Affect   Unable to Perform Duties

Question 59

While visiting your grandmother you enter her house and see her lying on the ground unconscious. In which order would you perform the following options?

    A - Attempt to wake her and see if she is all right.

    B - Call 911 for emergency assistance.

    C - Begin CPR.

    D - Check for airway blockage, breathing and circulation.

a) A, C, D, B   b) A, D, C, B, C

c) A, D, B, C   d) D, B, C

Question 60

How confident are you with the decision you made above on a scale of 1 to 9, with 9 being the most confident?

    1   2   4   5   6   7   8   9

  Not Confident   Moderately Confident   Extremely Confident

Question 61

Which tool would most likely be used for breaking down a door?

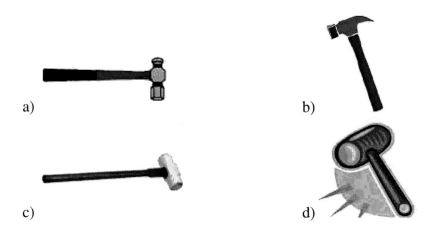

a)   b)

c)   d)

Question 62

One of your co-workers on the night shift has a tendency to arrive late to relieve the day shift. His actions do not affect you, but you know it bothers the firefighters who have to wait for him. What action should you take?

a) Inform the supervisor of the problem.

b) Let him know that he should arrive on time.

c) Tell the people who are bothered to report him to a supervisor.

d) Ignore the situation as you are not his supervisor and his actions do not bother you.

Question 63

While responding to a first aid call at a retirement home you are required to treat an 89-year-old man who is suffering from diabetic shock. The man is semi-conscious, but is shaking violently. There is foam coming from the his mouth. On a scale of 1 to 9, with 9 being the most severe, how distraught would you be?

	1	2	4	5	6	7	8	9	

Not distraught at all   Extremely distraught

Question 64

On a scale of 1 to 9, with 9 being unable to perform your duties, how would the above situation affect your job performance?

	1	2	4	5	6	7	8	9	

No Affect   Unable to Perform Duties

Question 65

Which of the following steps would you take if you were confronted with a paper fire in your back porch?

a) Pour water on the material.   b) Use an A-Class fire extinguisher.

c) Use a fire extinguisher labelled A + D.   d) Any of the above.

Question 66

How confident are you with the decision you made above on a scale of 1 to 9, with 9 being the most confident?

	1	2	4	5	6	7	8	9	

Not Confident   Moderately Confident   Extremely Confident

Question 67

What is the volume of the object below?

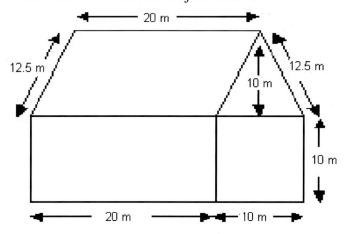

a) 3,000 m³

b) 3,500 m³

c) 2,500 m³

d) 4,000 m³

Question 68

While performing a safety inspection at a local bar you come across several serious infractions which warrant fines. The bar owner informs you that he is related to the Fire Chief. He provides identification confirming this. What action is appropriate?

a) Issue the fines and inform your captain of the situation.

b) Ignore the situation as the Fire Chief can handle any infractions.

c) Issue the fines and inform authorities about the Chief's involvement.

d) Either A or C would be appropriate.

Question 69

While working one winter you are dispatched to an emergency rescue attempt of a 7-year-old child who fell through the ice at the local pond. The child was under water for twenty minutes before he was finally pulled to safety. He has no pulse and is not breathing as you begin CPR. On a scale of 1 to 9, with 9 being the most severe, how distraught would you be?

              1   2   4   5   6   7   8   9

Not distraught at all   Extremely distraught

Question 70

On a scale of 1 to 9, with 9 being unable to perform your duties, how would the above situation affect your job performance?

              1   2   4   5   6   7   8   9

No Affect   Unable to Perform Duties

Question 71

Which of the following are advantages that aluminium ladders have over wood ladders?

a) They are more likely to melt than wood ladders.

b) An aluminum ladder the same size as a wood ladder will be lighter.

c) They can be made taller than wood ladders.

d) Aluminium is more subject to rusting.

Question 72

How confident are you with the decision you made above on a scale of 1 to 9, with 9 being the most confident?

	1	2	4	5	6	7	8	9	

Not Confident   Moderately Confident   Extremely Confident

Question 73

A man drove 350 km at a speed of 90 km per hour. If the total length of his journey is 500 km, and he wants to complete the journey within 5 hours, at what speed does he have to drive the rest of the distance at?

a) 142.8 km / hour   b) 136.4 km / hour

c) 133.5 km / hour   d) 128.6 km / hour

Question 74

While working, one of your co-workers asks you to donate $200 to a firefighter charity event. You feel you donate enough to charities at home, and don't feel comfortable donating any more money. What is an appropriate response?

a) Explain that you donate to charities at home and that you can't give anymore at this time.

b) Write a letter to the Chief stating that fundraising should not be allowed on the job.

c) Yell at your co-worker for being so rude to ask for such a large amount of money.

d) Donate the money anyway; it is for a good cause.

Question 75

You receive a call in the middle of the night for an elderly female who has stopped breathing in her sleep. By the time you arrive the female has no vital signs, and you are unable to resuscitate her. On a scale of 1 to 9, with 9 being the most severe, how distraught would you be?

	1	2	4	5	6	7	8	9	

Not distraught at all   Extremely distraught

Question 76

On a scale of 1 to 9, with 9 being unable to perform your duties, how would the above situation affect your job performance?

         1   2   4   5   6   7   8   9

No Affect   Unable to Perform Duties

Question 77

Which of the following order of options is the best way to handle a motor vehicle collision?

        A – Treat Shawna, who has severe bleeding from a head gash.

        B – Request an ambulance, the police and another pumper.

        C – Clear all the people away from the Honda on fire.

        D – Provide a detailed account to the investigating officer.

        E – Transport Kevin and Kelly to Mount Sinai hospital for minor treatment.

a) B, C, D, E, A   b) E, A, C, B, D

c) C, B, A, E, D   d) A, C, B, E, D

Question 78

How confident are you with the decision you made above on a scale of 1 to 9, with 9 being the most confident?

         1   2   4   5   6   7   8   9

 Not Confident   Moderately Confident   Extremely Confident

Question 79

Which of the following saws would most likely be used to cut through a piece of sheet metal?

a)

b)

c)   d)

Question 80

While in a burning building you encounter a child who is clinging to a handrail on a stairwell and is afraid to let go. Which of the following actions would be the most appropriate?

a) Call the child's mother into the house, as it will be easier for her to remove the child without incident.

b) Continue checking for other victims and return for the child afterward.

c) Pick up the child and carry him out of the building, willing or not.

d) Talk to the child to reduce the level of fear so he will come with you.

Question 81

Your captain gives you an order get a hose line up to the third floor of an apartment fire. You miscount the floors and deliver the hose line to the fourth floor. As a result, a family suffers smoke inhalation because it took too long for firefighters to reach them. They are treated and released from the hospital. On a scale of 1 to 9, with 9 being the most severe, how distraught would you be?

1	2	4	5	6	7	8	9

Not distraught at all   Extremely distraught

Question 82

On a scale of 1 to 9, with 9 being unable to perform your duties, how would the above situation affect your job performance?

1	2	4	5	6	7	8	9

No Affect   Unable to Perform Duties

Question 83

After a serious fire, you are required to shower and wash any clothing you were wearing. Which of the following would be the most important reason for doing this?

a) To maintain the equipment's lifespan.

b) To maintain a professional image to the public.

c) To relax and unwind after a stressful situation.

d) To eliminate any hazardous chemicals or contaminants that may have been picked up in the fire.

Question 84

How confident are you with the decision you made above on a scale of 1 to 9, with 9 being the most confident?

1	2	4	5	6	7	8	9

Not Confident   Moderately Confident   Extremely Confident

Question 85

In the example below the box has to be lifted 2 metres. If the box weighs 140 kg, how much effort is required to lift the box?

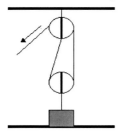

a) 140 kg

b) 70 kg

c) 280 kg

d) None of the above.

Question 86

You arrive on the scene of a drug overdose call. As your truck stops a police officer orders you to stay out of the house and rushes into it with his gun drawn. What action should you take?

a) Obey the officer's order and wait until he informs you that the situation is safe.

b) Assess the situation and, if you feel it is safe, enter the house.

c) Call the officer back to explain the situation to your captain.

d) Rush in anyway, this is a medical call and the person requires assistance.

Question 87

While attending a medical complaint for an elderly female who broke her hip in a fall, she continually asks for something to ease her pain. Any movement causes her to cry out in pain, but there is nothing you can prescribe to her on scene. On a scale of 1 to 9, with 9 being the most severe, how distraught would you be?

        1   2   4   5   6   7   8   9

Not distraught at all   Extremely distraught

Question 88

On a scale of 1 to 9, with 9 being unable to perform your duties, how would the above situation affect your job performance?

        1   2   4   5   6   7   8   9

No Affect   Unable to Perform Duties

Question 89

Which of the following factors are important to consider while enroute to a fire in progress?

a) What other emergency personnel may be required on the scene.

b) The best route to the fire.

c) Any potential dangers that may exist in the area.

d) All of the above.

Question 90

How confident are you with the decision you made above on a scale of 1 to 9, with 9 being the most confident?

	1	2	4	5	6	7	8	9

Not Confident   Moderately Confident   Extremely Confident

Question 91

Bill and Sue each had a collection of comic books. Bill told Sue, "If you give me 6 of your comic books, than I will have twice as many comics as you." Sue made the exact same statement. How many comics did each child have?

a) 16   b) 18

c) 20   d) 22

Question 92

After extinguishing a fire, the owners of the house approach you. They are very poor and request that you increase the damage estimates in your report so the insurance will provide enough money to meet their needs. Which actions below are appropriate?

a) Accuse the owners of fraud and begin a confrontation with them.

b) Fill the report out properly, but keep the owner's request to yourself as there was no harm done and no one needs to know.

c) Fill the report out properly without adjusting the estimated damages and report the incident to your captain.

d) Adjust the estimated damages up a little as these people are in real financial trouble.

Question 93

You are called to an elementary school for a first aid complaint. A child who is allergic to bees has been stung by one. When you arrive the child is shaking violently and there are hives breaking out on his shoulders and back. On a scale of 1 to 9, with 9 being the most severe, how distraught would you be?

	1	2	4	5	6	7	8	9

Not distraught at all   Extremely distraught

Question 94

On a scale of 1 to 9, with 9 being unable to perform your duties, how would the above situation affect your job performance?

| | 1 | 2 | 4 | 5 | 6 | 7 | 8 | 9 |

No Affect   Unable to Perform Duties

Question 95

While working at the station you receive a phone complaint from a citizen who states her stove caught fire while frying chicken. She is asking for advice. What is the proper order of the information below?

A – Alert the other family members to the damage.

B – Turn off the stove.

C – Pour water from the sink over the flame.

D – Do nothing and wait for the fire department to attend.

E – Cover the fire with a pot lid, or baking soda.

a) B, E, A, D   b) B, C, A, D

c) C, D   d) B, A, D

Question 96

How confident are you with the decision you made above on a scale of 1 to 9, with 9 being the most confident?

| | 1 | 2 | 4 | 5 | 6 | 7 | 8 | 9 |

Not Confident   Moderately Confident   Extremely Confident

Question 97

What is the primary use of this power tool?

a) Rounding and chipping wood.   b) Sharpening other tools.

c) Sanding wood, steel or plastic.   d) Fastening joints together.

Question 98

You find out that one of your co-workers is gay but has not told anyone else in the firehall. He has been on the job for 10 years and you have personally worked with him for 2 years. Which of the following actions is appropriate?

a) Approach him and advise him to tell the station of his sexual orientation.

b) Do not say anything and continue with the working relationship you have always had.

c) Write a letter to your union representative complaining about the situation.

d) Tell your fellow co-workers, as it is vital information to the job.

Question 99

You are dispatched to attend a medical complaint. A child was left unattended in a bath tub and was under water for a period of time. When you arrive the child is very pale and is not breathing. On a scale of 1 to 9, with 9 being the most severe, how distraught would you be?

		1	2	4	5	6	7	8	9	

Not distraught at all   Extremely distraught

Question 100

On a scale of 1 to 9, with 9 being unable to perform your duties, how would the above situation affect your job performance?

		1	2	4	5	6	7	8	9	

No Affect   Unable to Perform Duties

Question 101

While working one afternoon you receive a phone call from an unknown person who states that there will be a fire started at 75 Charles Street later this week. In which order would you perform the following actions?

A - Call the owners of 75 Charles Street.

B - Notify the police about the threat.

C - Notify your captain.

D - Increase routine patrols around the area during your inspections.

E - Be more vigilant about any emergency calls to this address.

a) C, B, D, E   b) B, A, D, E

c) A, D, E   d) B, D, E

Question 102

How confident are you with the decision you made above on a scale of 1 to 9, with 9 being the most confident?

| 1 | 2 | 4 | 5 | 6 | 7 | 8 | 9 |

Not Confident   Moderately Confident   Extremely Confident

Question 103

A firefighter is attempting to pry a steel door open with a crow bar. The door is manufactured to withstand a force of 400 kg. Due to space limitations, the firefighter is able to exert only 35 kg of effort. What would the minimum length of the following bar have to be in order to successfully open the door?

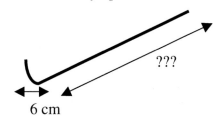

???

6 cm

a) 62.4 cm

b) 68.6 cm

c) 69.5 cm

d) 64.6 cm

Question 104

After extinguishing a fire, one of your co-workers asks if you can talk to the owners, who are pestering him with questions. He has already tried and is becoming frustrated and angry with them. Which of the following actions is appropriate?

a) Bring the matter to your captain immediately.

b) Agree to speak to the owners and inform your captain about your co-workers' poor judgment and self-control.

c) Inform your co-worker that he should be the one who finishes addressing the owner's concerns, as he is more familiar with the situation.

d) Agree to speak to the owners and attempt to address their concerns.

Question 105

While dispatched to a medical complaint for a homeless man in a back alley, you find the 45-year-old man stabbed to death inside a dumpster. On a scale of 1 to 9, with 9 being the most severe, how distraught would you be?

| 1 | 2 | 4 | 5 | 6 | 7 | 8 | 9 |

Not distraught at all   Extremely distraught

Question 106

On a scale of 1 to 9, with 9 being unable to perform your duties, how would the above situation affect your job performance?

1   2   4   5   6   7   8   9

No Affect   Unable to Perform Duties

Question 107

While walking along the street one afternoon you witness a man hit a woman over the head and steal her purse. The man takes off down the street and the woman falls unconscious to the ground. Citizens rush to help the woman. In which order would you perform the following actions?

A - Go to the woman and check her medical condition.

B - Attempt to catch the man

C – Have someone call 911.

D - Do nothing, as others in the area are assisting her.

E – Provide any First Aid or CPR as required.

a) B, A, C, D, E   b) A, C, E

c) B, D   d) A, C, E, B, D

Question 108

How confident are you with the decision you made above on a scale of 1 to 9, with 9 being the most confident?

1   2   4   5   6   7   8   9

Not Confident   Moderately Confident   Extremely Confident

Question 109

If a jackscrew handle is 45 cm long, and the screw pitch is 1/4 of a cm, how much effort is required to lift a weight of 4,500 kg?

a) 3.98 kg   b) 6.72 kg

c) 8.55 kg   d) 10.75 kg

Question 110

While on the scene of a serious fire you are ordered by your captain to break a door down and search a room for possible trapped victims. You feel the building is becoming too dangerous and want to leave. What is the best course of action?

a) Obey the order.

b) Inform the captain that you feel the building isn't safe and that you wish to leave.

c) Leave the building, as it is unsafe to stay.

d) Disregard the order, as it is not a safe situation.

Question 111

You are dispatched to back up another pumper at a serious fire. While enroute, you make a wrong turn and delay your arrival by several minutes. This puts the victims in the fire at added risk. On a scale of 1 to 9, with 9 being the most severe, how distraught would you be?

	1	2	4	5	6	7	8	9

Not distraught at all   Extremely distraught

Question 112

On a scale of 1 to 9, with 9 being unable to perform your duties, how would the above situation affect your job performance?

	1	2	4	5	6	7	8	9

No Affect   Unable to Perform Duties

Question 113

While actively fighting a serious apartment fire from the outside, the owner advises you that there was a homeless man who sometimes stays in the basement and may still be there. Due to concern that the fire may spread to an adjoining building, most of the attention is currently focused on the roof. There are presently no firefighters in the apartment, which has been evacuated. Which actions would be appropriate?

a) Continue focusing efforts on the roof.

b) Immediately inform your captain about the new information.

c) Enter the apartment and inspect the basement for the man.

d) Direct more of your efforts to the main floor so you can get access to the basement.

Question 114

How confident are you with the decision you made above on a scale of 1 to 9, with 9 being the most confident?

	1	2	4	5	6	7	8	9

Not Confident   Moderately Confident   Extremely Confident

Question 115

Which of the following tools could be used to tighten bolts?

a) Ratchet   b) Wrench

c) Both A and B   d) Neither A nor B

Question 116

You are assigned to the aerial tower and are responding to an apartment fire. While operating the tower, other firefighters fail to attach their safety belts, stating that the belts restrict their movement when reaching for victims. Training dictates that you have to use the safety belt while operating the tower. Which of the following choices is the best option to take?

a) Order your co-workers to use the safety belt and refuse to operate the apparatus without it.

b) Refuse to operate the tower and leave the scene.

c) Follow along with your co-workers and operate the tower without the safety belt.

d) Continue to use the safety belt as you were trained to do.

Question 117

While responding to a industrial accident at a factory, you are working on a man whose leg is pinned by some heavy debris. Every movement you make causes the man to scream out in intense pain. On a scale of 1 to 9, with 9 being the most severe, how distraught would you be?

$$1 \quad 2 \quad 4 \quad 5 \quad 6 \quad 7 \quad 8 \quad 9$$

Not distraught at all   Extremely distraught

Question 118

On a scale of 1 to 9, with 9 being unable to perform your duties, how would the above situation affect your job performance?

$$1 \quad 2 \quad 4 \quad 5 \quad 6 \quad 7 \quad 8 \quad 9$$

No Affect   Unable to Perform Duties

Question 119

One night while driving home you come across a house fire. You pull up out front and a woman yells that her husband ran inside a few minutes ago to get their children but hasn't returned. There is heavy smoke coming from the building and you can see flames inside the front door. You can see the husband lying on the ground just inside the door. In which order would you perform the following actions?

A - Search the building for the children.

B - Call 911 on your cell phone to request fire, police and ambulance assistance.

C - Grab a ladder from the side of the house to see if you can see the children through a window.

D - Do nothing and wait for properly-equipped firefighters.

E - Rush into the building to pull the man to safety.

a) E, A, B, C, D   b) E, B, C, D, A

c) B, D   d) B, C, D

Question 120

How confident are you with the decision you made above on a scale of 1 to 9, with 9 being the most confident?

	1	2	4	5	6	7	8	9

Not Confident   Moderately Confident   Extremely Confident

Question 121

In the diagram below two wheels attached by a belt drive have a 4:1 ratio. The smaller wheel has a 15 cm circumference. How fast would the smaller wheel turn if the larger one turned at a rate of 245 rpm?

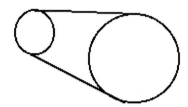

a) 980 rpm

b) 1,500 rpm

c) 61.25 rpm

d) 150 rpm

Question 122

You are a rookie on the job. While working with a senior firefighter he performs an action you do not understand or agree with. What is the best solution below?

a) Immediately correct the senior firefighter so any bystanders don't become confused or concerned.

b) Inform a supervisor about the senior officer's mistake.

c) Privately talk to the senior officer about the action taken, your concerns and lack of understanding, after the situation is over.

d) Disregard the situation, as it is not that important.

Question 123

You are dispatched to a medical complaint involving a 3-month-old infant. The child fell off a change table and landed on her head. When you arrive the baby is unconscious and its breathing is laboured. The baby is also shaking uncontrollably. On a scale of 1 to 9, with 9 being the most severe, how distraught would you be?

	1	2	4	5	6	7	8	9

Not distraught at all   Extremely distraught

Question 124

On a scale of 1 to 9, with 9 being unable to perform your duties, how would the above situation affect your job performance?

       1   2   4   5   6   7   8   9

No Affect   Unable to Perform Duties

Question 125

Your neighbour informs you that his wife accidentally cut herself on the arm and is bleeding quite heavily. He doesn't know what to do. Which of the following would be the best course of action?

a) Tell your friend to apply pressure to the cut until the bleeding stops.

b) Go and examine the cut to see if you can provide any direct assistance.

c) Tell your neighbour to call 911 for emergency help.

d) Advise your neighbour to take your wife to a clinic to have the cut treated.

1)	C	43)	B	85)	B
2)	D	44)	C	86)	A
5)	C	47)	D	89)	D
7)	C	49)	B	91)	B
8)	D	50)	A	92)	C
11)	A	53)	C	95)	A
13)	B	55)	A	97)	C
14)	C	56)	C	98)	B
17)	B	59)	B	101)	A
19)	D	61)	C	103)	B
20)	C	62)	D	104)	D
23)	D	65)	D	107)	D
25)	A	67)	A	109)	A
26)	B	68)	A	110)	A
29)	A	71)	B	113)	B
31)	C	73)	B	115)	C
32)	A	74)	A	116)	D
35)	D	77)	C	119)	B
37)	D	79)	D	121)	A
38)	C	80)	C	122)	C
41)	D	83)	D	125)	B

Questions 6, 12, 18, 24, 30, 36, 42, 48, 54, 60, 66, 72, 78, 84, 90, 96, 102, 108, 114, 120
When answering Confidence questions you should be attempting to answer them with a high degree of confidence. If your scores are consistently low (below 7 – 9) you will have difficulty passing these forms of tests. Your answers should be consistently 8 or 9.

Below are question groups that have similar themes. Your answers should be fairly consistent within the groups. If you find your answers aren't consistent, you will have difficulty passing the test. Don't worry if you have one or two stray marks per group, but if you don't see a range of marks within 2 or 3 numbers, then you will have difficulty with the exams.

Write your answer selection for each of the following questions in the appropriate groups.

Group 1a - seizures/shock									Range
3		33		63		93		123	

Group 1b - needs to be a low number (1-2)									Range
4		34		64		94		124	

Group 2a - drowning							Range
9		39		69		99	

Group 2b – needs to be a low number (1-2)							Range
10		40		70		100	

Group 3a – dealing with death							Range
15		45		75		105	

Group 3b – needs to be a low number (1-2)							Range
16		46		76		106	

Group 4a – errors on your part							Range
21		51		81		111	

Group 4b – needs to be a low number (1-2)							Range
22		52		82		112	

Group 5a – patient in pain							Range
27		57		87		117	

Group 5b – needs to be a low number (1-2)							Range
28		58		88		118	

Question 1

First determine the total area of the canvas by multiplying the dimensions: 3m x 5m = 15 square meters. If she has already painted 2/5's of the canvas, then she has painted 6 square meters of the canvas (15 x 2 / 5 = 6). To see what is remaining, subtract the total size of the canvas by that which is already painted (15 – 6 = 9 m²).

Question 2

None of the options would be acceptable. You should not involve the children in activity that may lead to harm, the private living quarters of the firefighters on the job is unavailable to the public, and it is inappropriate to remove equipment from the trucks in case an emergency call occurs.

Question 5

It would be improper to disregard your surroundings while you are driving to an emergency call. You should slow the truck a little and drive cautiously. Delaying an arrival by a couple of seconds is a far better option than running the risk of hitting a child and not making it to the fire at all. There is no need to take a different route, as it will delay your arrival. While traveling to an emergency call, your lights and sirens should remain activated to warn motorists and pedestrians that you are driving quickly through the area.

Question 7

A plumb bob is used to determine a vertical line.

Question 8

Acting dishonestly would be inappropriate behaviour as you were left with the care of the tool and you are responsible for its loss. Either purchasing a new tool for Captain Gordon, or at least letting him know what happened to it, would be suitable actions to take in this situation.

Question 11

D – A – C – E – B

Your primary concern is to get the baby to safety as quickly as possible. Opening the door would be the quickest means of accomplishing this, and should be attempted first. The next quickest means to reach the baby would be to break a window.

Question 13

The formula for the mechanical advantage of inclined planes is:

Effort x Length = Resistance x Height

Effort x 12 = 150 x 3
Effort x 12 = 450
Effort = 450 / 12   (isolate effort)
Effort = 37.5 kg

Question 14

You should advise on the proper placement of the equipment and inform a supervisor only if the problem persists. You should not be talking about co-workers behind their backs in a negative manner. It would be best to try and rectify the situation without getting the captain involved. You are not the supervisor and should not chastise the worker.

Question 17

One of your first priorities when you arrive at an emergency scene is to ensure the safety of yourself, your co-workers and any victims in the area. Unplugging the toaster will eliminate the threat of electric shock.

Question 19

1 hour and 45 minutes works out to 105 minutes (60 + 45). Simply multiply 25% to this total for the answer.

105 x 0.25 = 26.25 = 26 ¼ minutes or 26 minutes and 15 seconds.
Remember that there are 60 seconds in a minute, so a quarter of a minute is 15 seconds.

Question 20

You should inform your captain of what you found and where you found it. Always be careful when handling money found at scenes. If it belongs to Lance, your captain will make sure it gets to him, and if someone else comes looking for it, your captain will be aware of it and be able to return the money to the rightful owner.

Question 23

It would be important to perform all three acts before breaking a door. You should check for signs of smoke and feel the door for heat to make sure there is no fire on the other side of the door. You should also be prepared for fire. Standing to the side of the door before breaking it open will put you out of harm's way, in case there is an explosion, or serious flames, behind the door.

Question 25

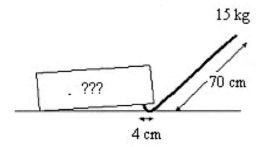

15 kg

70 cm

???

4 cm

The formula for the mechanical advantage of a lever is:

Effort x (Distance 1) = Resistance x (Distance 2)

15 x (70) = Resistance x (4)
1,050 = Resistance x 4
1,050 / 4 = Resistance   (divide both sides by 4 to isolate resistance)
262.5 = Resistance

Question 26

You should approach the officer, identify yourself and ask if she needs assistance. The officer has been on the scene for longer, is familiar with the situation, and has been trained to handle accidents like these. It is important to address the immediate needs of the injured parties.

Option 29

B – D – C – E

At this stage, the driver's life is in danger and you have the opportunity to save it if you act quickly. Your first priority is to get yourself and those around you to a safe distance. Calling 911 and getting emergency personnel dispatched is very important and should be the next step. It would be improper to fight such a serious fire with a small fire extinguisher. You should stay back from the danger and wait until the arrival of trained personnel with the proper equipment to handle the emergency.

Question 31

First determine the area of the entire floor. The formula for the area of a rectangle is:

A = length x width
= 40 x 25
= 1,000 m^2

The area of the run on the floor is determined by the following formula:

Area = π r^2
= 3.14 x 2^2 (radius = ½ diameter)
= 3.14 x 4
= 12.56 m^2 x 3 =   37.68 m^2

Subtract the total area of the room by the area that the floor is covering.
1,000 – 37.68 = 962.32 m^2

Question 32

You should inform your friend to contact media relations if he needs more information, as you can't talk about it. Information you reveal may compromise the investigation or damage the reputation of the fire department. There is no need to be rude, as you were approached in a friendly manner. Simply inform him that you are unable to comment on the situation.

Question 35

You should disregard the dog and continue to fight the fire. Fighting a house fire is a very dangerous situation. Concern for the safety of yourself and others while attempting to gain control of the blaze is far more important than risking your life for an animal.

Question 37

A first step you can take is to eliminate the brackets by multiplying 2 to both Y and 15.

$$2 (Y + 15) - 75 = 225$$
$$2Y + 30 - 75 = 225$$

Next subtract 30 from each side and add 75 to each side to begin isolating Y.

$$2Y + 30 - 30 - 75 + 75 = 225 - 30 + 75$$
$$2Y = 270$$

Finally, divide both sides by 2 to isolate Y.

$$2Y / 2 = 270 / 2$$
$$Y = 135$$

Question 38

You should ignore the youth and tend to the unconscious female. Your primary concern is the medical issue. The youth's complaint can be dealt with after the victim is treated.

Question 41

You should never use water, or a water-based fire extinguisher, when attempting to extinguish an electrical fire. Simply removing the electrical source doesn't guarantee that the fire will be extinguished. Although smothering the flame is one means of putting out an electrical fire, there are other options available, including using a chemical-based fire extinguisher.

Question 43

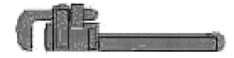

Pipe Wrench
Grips round objects such as pipes and steel rods.
Adjusts to accommodate various sizes.

Question 44

The firefighters would not be violating any procedures. There is nothing wrong with bringing in a surprise for the captain. Informing your captain of the surprise may create resentment among your co-workers. There is no need for the captain of the fire station to know about the cake.

Question 47

It would be important to notify your co-workers about the needles so they can search the victim in case he was carrying more. Getting poked with a hypodermic needle is a very real threat to firefighters. Searching the area for other needles is important because, if found, they can be disposed of safely so others don't get injured. Information from the victim's friend may be helpful for the medical treatment that is required.

Question 49

One of the best ways to answer this problem is to determine which gears will turn the same way. Any two gears touching will spin in opposite directions.

Group 1 – A, C, E
Group 2 – B, D, F

The rpm for gears is affected by the size and their number of teeth. If a smaller gear is being turned by a larger gear, it will turn faster. If there are a different number of teeth in each gear, they will turn at different speeds.

Question 50

You should inform your supervisor immediately. The fire department has already been informed and action must be taken. You should only rush to the house to investigate the situation with your entire truck and equipment. Your captain will need to be made aware of the situation so this can take place.

Question 53

You should call the police immediately. Firefighters aren't trained to deal with these types of emergencies. The police should be called to handle the situation and enter the house.

Question 55

First determine how many slices of pizza there are.
Pizza 1 = 18 slices
Pizza 2 = 27 slices (18 x 1.5)
Pizza 3 = 30 slices (27 + 3)
Total slices = 75 (18 + 27 + 30)

Next determine how much Groups A and B ate.
Group A = 75 x 1/3 = 25 slices
Group B = 75 x 0.4 = 30 slices
Remaining slices = 20 (75 – 55)

Finally, set up an algebraic equation to solve how many slices Group D ate. Let Y represent the amount that group D ate. Therefore, 2Y would be the amount that Group C ate.
2Y + Y = 20
3Y = 20
Y = 20 / 3
Y = 6.7 slices   Group D ate approximately 6.7 of the remaining 20 slices.

Question 56
The diary is personal and private property not meant to be read by strangers. The diary belongs to someone in the house and is not lost property. There is no mention of a fire investigation or any logical reason why your captain has a right to read through the diary.

Question 59
A – D – C – B – C
This is a standard first aid/CPR question about prioritizing actions. While performing CPR alone, your first step is to attempt to wake the victim. If you are unsuccessful you then check her airway, breathing and circulation (remember the A, B, C's). If you have to perform CPR alone you should go through one complete cycle, call for help, then continue CPR until help arrives.

Question 61

Sledge Hammer
Heavy-duty instrument primarily used for breaking concrete, driving posts, etc.

Question 62
You should ignore the situation as you are not his supervisor and his actions do not bother you. This is a problem at the station that doesn't affect you. You should not be speaking negatively about your co-workers behind their backs. You are not the man's supervisor and neither is it your place to inform the supervisor.

Question 65
A paper-based fire can be effectively handled by pouring water on the source or using any fire extinguisher with an A-Class label. This includes extinguishers with multiple ratings.

Question 67
To calculate the volume of the cube (bottom portion), use the following formula:

Volume = length x width x height
= 20 x 10 x 10
= 200 x 10
= 2,000 m^3

To calculate the volume of the triangular top portion, first find the area of the triangle front.

Area = ½ base x height
= ½ (10 x 10)
= ½ x 100
= 50 m^2

The volume is then calculated by multiplying the area x the length of the roof for a volume of 1000 m^3 (50 x 20). The total volume of the object is therefore 3,000 m^3 (2,000 bottom + 1,000 top).

Question 68
You should issue the fines and inform your captain of the situation. Letting the man go with a caution is unprofessional as you would be giving the man a break simply because he knows the fire chief. There is no information that the fire chief is aware of the bar owner's infractions.

Question 71
Aluminum ladders the same size as a wood ladder would be lighter, more durable and less likely to catch fire.

Question 73
The man has already driven for 3.9 hours (350 / 90 = 3.888 or 3.9 hours). He therefore has to drive 150 km (500 – 350) in 1.1 hours (5 – 3.9). This works out to 136.4 km / hour (150 / 1.1 = 136.3636 or 136.4).

Question 74
If you feel that you don't want to donate money to the cause you must have the conviction to say no. There may be many charities that benefit from these collections, but you can simply state you do not wish to donate at this time. It is all right to say no.

Question 77
C – B – A – E – D
You have to prioritize your actions when answering these types of questions. The first step is to make sure the area is safe for the victims involved in the accident. As the area is brought under control you should request whatever additional help you feel is required so it can be enroute while you continue to work. As you begin performing first aid, you should prioritize the people with the life-threatening injuries first, followed by those with minor injuries. Providing a detailed account would occur after medical emergencies are handled.

Question 79

Hack Saw
Cuts through metal sheets, piping, plastics, etc.

Question 80
Your primary concern is getting the child out of the house and to safety. There would not be time to reason with a frightened child in a burning building. If you lose sight of the child he may run into another room and hide. You would not want to bring another civilian into a dangerous situation.

Question 83
Firefighters are often subject to harsh and dangerous chemicals when they put out fires. These chemicals can have cancerous agents and should be washed off as soon as possible. The other answer choices may be correct, but the main reason for showering is to wash away the chemicals.

Question 85

The mechanical advantage in this pulley is 2:1 as the weight is evenly distributed across two ropes. This will reduce the weight by 50% but will also reduce the height of the lift by 50%. You will need twice as much rope to cover the same distance, or 4 metres of rope to lift the object 2 meters. The amount of effort required is 70 kg, as the mechanical advantage, as stated above, is 2:1.

Question 86

You should obey the officer's order and wait until he informs you that the situation is safe. It is obvious that there is a dangerous situation for which you are not trained to deal. The officer would not be able to explain everything at this time.

Question 89

While you are traveling to an emergency you should be concentrating on the quickest route to the scene, thinking of what other assistance you may need in terms of equipment or material, and considering any dangers that may exist on the scene. Thinking of all three factors could allow you to get there in the quickest time, place the vehicle in the safest area and order any other assistance, such as tow trucks or police, as required.

Question 91

This question will require an algebraic equation. We will assume that "Y" represents the number of comic books that both children have. If we increase "Y" by 12, then it must equal twice the number of Y – 12. The equation will look like this:

$Y + 6 = 2(Y - 6)$	Brackets have to be handled first.
$Y + 6 = 2Y - 12$	Next, collect like terms by subtracting y from both sides.
$6 = 2Y - Y - 12$	Next, add 24 to both sides.
$6 + 12 = Y$	
$18 = Y$	"Y" represents the number of comic books that each child has. Each child has 18 comic books.

Question 92

As a professional you must act honestly. You should fill out the report properly without adjusting the estimated damages and inform your captain about the incident. Your captain may have additional information and there could be more to this fire than you realize, such as a pending arson investigation. Keeping your captain well informed would be a good idea. There is no need to begin a confrontation with the owners at this stage.

Question 95

B – E – A – D

Water should not be poured on a grease fire as it will cause the fire to spread. Action should be taken to eliminate the blaze.

Question 97

Belt Sander

Sands wood, steel or plastic. The sheets run through the machine, which are embedded with various abrasives. A back and forth motion is used.

Question 98

There is no need to say anything. The information has been secret for a decade and hasn't affected his work performance. It is his right to keep his sexual orientation private if he wishes. A letter to the union would be inappropriate as well. You should simply continue to work as you always have.

Question 101

C – B – D – E

Your first priority in this situation is to notify your captain about the situation and threat. Your captain is most likely going to inform the police and arrange increased patrols in the area. You should also be more vigilant about any potential emergency calls to that address.

Question 103

The formula for the mechanical advantage of a lever is:

Effort x (Distance 1) = Resistance x (Distance 2)

35 kg x (Distance 1) = 400 kg x (6 cm)
35 x Distance = 2,400
Distance = 2,400 / 35 (divide both sides by 35 to isolate the distance)
Distance = 68.6 cm

Question 104

You should agree to speak to the owners and attempt to address their concerns. Working as a firefighter requires teamwork. Your co-worker is asking for assistance with a situation he is having a difficult time handling. If this is a one-time affair, then there is no need to get your supervisor involved. The fact that your co-worker came and asked for assistance demonstrates that he exercised excellent judgment.

Question 107

A – C – E – B – D

Your primary concern should be the safety and well-being of the victim. While you are assisting the victim, you should detail someone else to call 911 in order to have the police respond, as well as an ambulance if it is required. You should also provide any First Aid or CPR that is required. Doing nothing is not an option, and chasing after the man could occur but not at the expense of neglecting the victim.

Question 109
First determine the circumference of the arc that the screw handle will make.

$$c = 2 (\pi) (r)$$
$$= 2 (3.14) (45)$$
$$= 6.28 (45)$$
$$= 282.6 \text{ cm}$$

Next determine the mechanical advantage that the jackscrew provides.

M.A. = circumference / screw pitch
$$= 282.6 \div 1/4$$
$$= 282.6 \times 4 \quad \text{(when dividing by fractions, multiply by the}$$
$$= 1130.4 \quad \text{reciprocal)}$$

Lastly, calculate the effort required to lift the weight.

Resistance = M.A. x effort
$$4,500 = 1130.4 \times \text{effort}$$
$$4,500 / 1130.4 = \text{effort}$$
$$3.98 \text{ kg} = \text{effort}$$

Question 110
You should obey the order. In emergency situations, orders have to be followed. If you felt the captain was missing some information then you should inform him or her. This scenario doesn't indicate that the captain is lacking any information. The two of you are in the exact same position. You have to obey the orders.

Question 113
You should immediately inform your captain about the new information. Your primary goal as a firefighter is to protect life. As soon as you are made aware that there is, potentially, a life in danger, you should immediately inform your captain so that a coordinated effort can be implemented to help save the man. Doing something on your own is an inappropriate act, as is neglecting the information.

Question 115

Both wrenches and ratchets are commonly used for tightening and loosening bolts.

Question 116
You should continue to use the safety belt as you were trained to do so, as you are sure of yourself in its use. You would not be able to leave the situation as it is an emergency and you are not the commanding officer of the men.

Question 119
E – B – C – D – A

The danger the man is in should be your immediate concern. In most cases, you should never enter a burning building without the proper equipment, but if the victim is visible and you can rush in and grab him. It would be worth the risk to do so. Afterward, you should immediately call 911 and get the proper personnel on the scene to handle the emergency. You should not rush into the house to do a search for the children unprepared. It would be appropriate to see if you can find them from outside the house.

Question 121
Because the larger wheel is four times the size of the smaller one, every time the larger wheel has one complete revolution, the smaller wheel has to have four. Simply multiply 4 times the number of revolutions the larger wheel has per minute to determine the speed of the smaller wheel.

$$4 \times 245 = 980 \text{ rpm}$$

Question 122
You should speak privately with the senior officer about the action taken, as well as your concern and lack of understanding, after the situation. You should not disregard the fact that you don't understand what is happening. It would not make sense to go above your co-worker's head, and correcting your co-worker in public could lead to animosity between yourself and your co-worker.

Question 125
You should go and examine the cut to see if you can provide any direct assistance. As a firefighter, it is your duty to provide emergency assistance to people in distress 24 hours a day, 7 days a week. You should immediately go and offer first aid assistance.